T H E L A B O R B O Y C O T T

A BIBLIOGRAPHY

Emanuel Stein - Director

Staff

Delia Randall
Jesse Prussin

Prepared under the auspices

of   the

U. S. WORKS PROGRESS ADMINISTRATION

Official Project No. 165-97-6999

Works Project No. APN-6073-1040

New York, 1936

Second Edition 1938

Mimeographed by

Official Project 465-97-3-18.

Reprinted by CROFTON PUBLISHING CORPORATION
Post Office Box 28
Newton, Massachusetts 02168

ISBN 0-89020-005-X

FOREWORD

Properly understood, the boycott as carried on by organized labor is an integral part of its tactics and cannot be completely isolated from the strike, especially the sympathetic strike, the picket, or other labor tactics. The purpose of picketing is usually two-fold: (1) To inform would-be workers that a strike is in progress and to persuade them not to act as strike-breakers; (2) to induce prospective customers not to patronize the 'struck' establishment. It is this latter phase which is commonly called boycotting; hence, we must consider picketing in a study of boycotts. Moreover, a refusal to work on non-union materials, or a threat to strike against an employer dealing with a boycotted firm must always be included, since both tactics are calculated to curtail the market of the boycotted firm. Injunctions, too, must be brought in, since many injunctions have been directed against boycotting activities. A complete bibliography, then, would have to include such tactics as the picket and the strike.

From purely practical considerations, however, it was thought wise to issue a bibliography solely on boycotts, and to supplement it later with additional bibliographies on picketing, etc., recognizing that some material is contained here which belongs more appropriately in another category and that a certain amount of overlapping is inevitable. In addition, the boycott involved in attempting to curtail an employer's prospective labor supply, in ways other than picketing, will also be the subject of separate bibliographical treatment. Here, we are concerned chiefly with the attempt to curtail the sale of employer's goods.

The present bibliography is divided into the following sections.

1. Books and Pamphlets, arranged alphabetically by authors.

2. Periodicals, arranged chronologically. The chronological treatment was preferred since periodical literature reflects better, or at least more extensively than books and pamphlets, important current issues. It is interesting to note the large number of periodical articles appearing shortly after the decision in the Danbury Hatters' Case.

3. Documents, arranged alphabetically.

4. Statutes, arranged by States.

5. Court decisions, arranged alphabetically and by States, the latter in order to assist the student concerned with labor law in particular states.

The staff members who cooperated in the preparation of this bibliography were: Miss Delia Randall and Mr. Jesse Prussin. Miss Estelle Muraskin and Mr. Peter Hagan helped in checking many of the items.

Emanuel Stein

Sept., 1936

PART   ONE

BOOKS AND PAMPHLETS

Allen, Henry J.   The party of the Third Part. Story of the Kansas In-
                         dustrial Relations Court. N. Y. Harper & Bros. 1921.

Beach, Charles Fishk   Commentaries on Law of Injunctions as determined by the
                         courts and statutes of England and the U. S. Albany.
                         H. B. Parsons, 1895.

Beck, J. M.;   Application of the Sherman Anti-Trust Law to labor
Light, J. H.;   boycotts: Oral Arguments made before the Supreme Court
Beach, J. K.;   of the United States: in the case of Loewe et al. v. Lawlor
Davenport, D.   et al. New York Anti-American Boycott Association, 1908.

Beckner, Earl R.   A history of labor legislation in Illinois. Chicago,
                         Univ. of Chicago Press, 1929.

Berman, Edward   Labor disputes and the President of the United States.
                         New York, Col. Univ., 1924.

Berman, Edward   Labor and the Sherman Act. Table of cases, see also
                         Appen. C. New York and London, Harper & Bros., 1930.

Bolen, George Lewis   Getting a living: the injunction in labor disputes.
                         New York, McMillan Co., 1903.

Brissenden, Paul   The labor injunction. New York, Academy of Political
                         Science, 1933.

Bryan, James W.   The development of the English Law of Conspiracy. For
                         combination of labor see pp. 115-158. Baltimore, 1909.

                         Buck's Stove and Range Co., injunction suit and contempt
                         proceedings: a compilation of the reports of the executive
                         council and Samuel Gompers to the Convention of the Ameri-
                         can Federation of Labor. Nov. 8-20, 1909, together with
                         the report of the Committee on the President's report.
                         Report of the Committee on Boycotts and the Vice-presi-
                         dent's address. Washington, American Federation of Labor,
                         1910.

Burns, W. G.   The Pullman Boycott: a complete history of the R. R.
                         strike.   St. Paul, McGill Printing Co., 1894.

Clark, Lindley   The law of the employment of labor. New York, MacMillan
Daniel   Co., 1911.

Cagley, Thomas Sydenham — The law of strikes, lockouts, and labor organizations. For "Strikes as conspiracies - boycotts - picketing - black-listing." see pp. 247-295. Washington, D. C., W. H. Lawdermilk & Co., 1894.

Cooke, F. H. — The law of trade and labor combinations as applicable to boycotts, strikes, trade conspiracies, pools, monopolies, and trusts. Chicago. Callaghan, 1898.

Cooke, Fred H. — The law of combinations, monopolies and labor unions. Chicago.

Commons, John Rogers — A Documentary History of Industrial America. Vol. 3 & 4. For early boycott cases; all reports to 1842. Also 6-10. Cleveland, 1910.

Commons, John R. — History of labor in the United States. New York, 1935.

Commons, John R. — Principles of labor legislation: see chap. 11 (2); chap. 3, also table of cases cited. New York. Harper & Bros., 1920.

Delaney, John H. — "If you see it in the Sun, it's not so." Typographical Union No. 6's reply to the statements appearing in the N. Y. Sun. New York. 1899?

Drew, Walter — The boycott. Also published as Educational Bulletin No. 15 National Association of Manufacturers in U. S. A. New York. 1910. New York. Ahearn, 1909.

Eddy, Arthur J. — The law of combinations. Chicago. Callaghan & Co., 1901.

Edwards, Alba M. — The labor legislation of Connecticut. New York American Economics Association: V. S. - Third Series, 1907.

Ellingwood, Albert Russell and Whitney Combs — The Government and Labor. New York. Shaw Co., 1926.

Frankfurter, Felix and Nathan Greene — The labor injunction. New York. MacMillan & Co., 1930.

Fitch, John A. — The Steel workers. (General and Boycotts.) New York. Charities Publications Committee, 1911.

Groat, George Gorham — Trade Unions and the law in New York, a study of some of the legal phases of labor organizations. New York. Columbia University Press, MacMillan Co., agents, 1905.

Groat, George G. — Attitude of American Courts in labor cases. New York. 1911.

Gompers, Samuel — Labor in Europe and America. New York. 1909.

Huebner, Grover G.   Boycotting, Madison. (Wisconsin Free Library Commission,
                         Legislative Reference Dept. Comparative Legislation Bull'
                         No. 9.) 1906.

Harker, Oliver   The contempt cases against the labor leaders and the power
Albert   of the President to pardon. Urbana, III. University of
                         Illinois, 1912.

Hunter, Wiles Robert   The Crisis - the unions - and the courts. The tyranny of
                         injunctions - the power of unity. Chicago. S. A. Block,
                         1909.

Knaus, Henry   Judicial usurpation, an open letter to Congress showing
                         this, in the injunctions in labor disputes. Chicago.
                         1908.

Laidler, Harry   Boycotts and the labor struggle. Introduction by H. R.
Wellington   Seager. New York. John Lane Co., 1914.

Laidler, Harry W.   The law of the boycott. (In: Orth. S.P. Readings on the
                         relations of Government to property and industry, pp. 485-
                         497.) 1915.

League for Indus-   Millions against one. A conspiracy to crush the open shop.
trial Rights   Connecticut. Danbury Medical Print Co., 1904.

League for Indus-   The boycott and public opinion. Editorial comment on the
trial Rights   recent unanimous decisions of the United States Supreme
                         Court. New York.Anti-Boycott Association, 1906.

League for Indus-   Bulletin of Recent Decisions. New York. American Anti-
trial Rights   Boycott Association. February, 1908.

                         Liberty and the boycott. Institute of Social Economics.
                         Lecture Bulletin, V. 3, No. 6. New York. 1899.

Loewe, D. E. & Co.   United States Circuit Court, Loewe or Danbury Hatters'
v. Lawlor, M. and   case. Narrative statement of evidence. Arguments of
others   Messrs. Davenport and Merritt. Summary of arguments of
                         defendents counsel. Charge of Judge James P. Platt and
                         to the jury. New York American Anti-Boycott Association.
                         1909.

Lord, Arthur   The writ of injunction in labor disputes. Arguments of
                         Arthur Lord before the Joint Special Committee on Labor
                         of the Massachusetts Legislature. New York American
                         Anti-Boycott Association, 1910.

Martin, W. A.   A treatise on the law of labor union, containing a consi-
                         deration of the law relating to trade disputes in all its
                         phases, internal administration of unions, unions labels,
                         and a collection of approved forms of pleadings injunc-
                         tions and restraining orders. Washington D. C.
                         J. Byrne and Co., 1910.

Mason, A. T.   Organized labor and the law. Durham, N.C. Duke University
                           Press, 1925.

Merritt, Walter G.   The neglected side of trade unions-the boycott. New York.
                           American Anti-Boycott Association, 1903.

Merritt, Walter G.   The open shop and industrial liberty. New York League for
                           Industrial Rights, 1922.

Merritt, Walter G.   History of the League for Industrial Rights. New York
                           League for Industrial Rights, 1925.

Mitchell, John   Speech delivered by John Mitchell at the Toronto Convention
                           of the Federation of Labor, November 19th, 1909, in support
                           of the report of the Committee on Boycott. Toronto.
                           American Federation of Labor, 1909

Mongold, William   The boycott as a means of Social Control. Chicago. 1911.
Christopher

Moses, Jacob M.   The law as applicable to strikes-boycotts. Pp. 18-20.
                           Prize thesis University of Maryland, 1895. Baltimore.
                           King Bros., 1895.

Oakes, Edwin   The law of organized labor and industrial conflicts. New
Stacey   York. Lawyers Co-operative Pub. Co., 1927.

Public Policy   Labor capital and the public. A discussion between employees,
                           employers and the public. Boycott against the employer per-
                           petually enjoined. Judge John Hunt Sup. Ct. San Francisco.
                           Pp. 119-138. Chicago. The Public Policy Pub. Co., 1905.

Ralston, Jackson, W.   Use and Abuse of injunction in trade disputes. Phila. 1910.

Ripley, William Z.   Strikes and boycotts. Cambridge, Mass. 1910

Schaffner, Margaret   Effect of the recent decisions on boycotts. Philadelphia.
Anna   American Academy of Political and Soc. Science No. 599. 1910.

Spedden, Ernest   The Trade Union Label. Dissertation at the John Hopkins
Radcliffe   University. Baltimore. John Hopkins Press, 1909.

                           Spies in the Trade Unions. Gerard, Kansas. J. A. Wayland,
                           1904

American Federation   Statement and evidence in support of petition against U. S.
of Labor   Steel Corporation. Washington D. C. 1910.

Stimson, Frederick   Handbook to the labor law of the United States. New York,
Jessup   1896.

Stockton, Frank T.   The Closed Shop in American trade unions. Baltimore. 1911.

Thornton, William
W.   A treatise on combination in restraint of trade. Cincin-
                            nati. W. H. Anderson Co., 1928.

                            United States: Supreme Court. Unanimous decision of the
                            U. S. Supreme Court in the case of Loewe v. Lawlor, hold-
                            ing that the Sherman Anti-Trust Law applies to labor com-
                            binations as well as those of capital. New York. Ameri-
                            can Anti-Boycott Association, 1908.

Waring, Luther Hess   The law and the gospel of labor. "Boycott." pp. 49-59.
                            New York and Washington D. C. Neale Publishing Co., 1907.

Witte, Edwin E.   Government in Labor Disputes. New York and London.
                            McGraw Hill Book Co., 1932.

Welman, Leo   The boycott in American Trade Unions. Also, John Hopkins
                            University series in historical and political science, se-
                            ries 34, no. 1. Baltimore. John Hopkins University
                            Press, 1915.

PART II

A. PERIODICAL LITERATURE

ARRANGED CHRONOLOGICALLY

Periodical literature provides a good source of informatiom on all subjects of importance and nation-wide interest. In compiling this bibliography a thorough search was made of all well known legal periodicals, together with those of interest to the general reader. Sources found to be of great assistance and to which thanks are given, were: Mr. Hermann H. B. Meyer's "Select list of references on boycotts and injunctions in labor disputes." Jones' Index to legal periodicals and law library journals, Law and Labor, Readers' Guide to periodicals, Poole's Index to periodical literature and the Catalogue Division of the Columbia University N. Y. C., and the New York Public Library, as well as others.

****

1880

Godkin, E. L., "Genesis of Boycotts", <u>Nation</u> (1880) Vol. XXXI. Pp. 437-438.

1884

Thompson, D., "Injunctions against Criminal Acts", <u>Amer. Law Rev.</u> (July-Aug., 1884) Vol. XVIII. Pp. 599-617.

1885

"Boycotting", <u>Justice of the Peace</u> (Oct. 31, 1885) Vol. XLIX. Pp. 689-691.

"Boycotts", <u>Bradstreet's</u> (Dec. 19, 1885) Vol. XII. Pp. 394-397.

1886

Atkins, Thos S., "The Criminality of Boycotting", <u>Va. Law Jour.</u> (DEc., 1886) Vol. X. Pp. 707-709.

Hammond, Wm. A., "Evolution of the Boycott", <u>Forum</u> (June, 1886) Vol. I. Pp. 369-376.

Mason, Jas. M., "The Legal Aspect of the Strike and the Boycott", <u>Kan. Law Jour.</u> (June 12, 1886) Vol. III. Pp. 273-279.

Stephen, J. Fitzjames, "On the Suppression of Boycotting", <u>Nineteenth Century</u> (1886) Vol. XX. P. 765.

Thacher, D., "Boycotting", <u>New Englander</u> (Dec., 1886) Vol. XLV. Pp. 1038-1042.

Vinton, A. D., "History of Boycotting", <u>Mag. of Western History</u> (1886) Vol. V. Pp. 211-224.

1887

Atkins, Thos. S., "The Law of Conspiracy - Boycotting", Va. Law Journal (June, 1887) Vol. XI. Pp. 324-331.

Becker, T. C., "Boycotting, Is It Criminal?", N. Y. State Bar Ass'n Reports (1887) Vol. X. P. 148.

Bingham, Clifford, "Strikes and Boycotts as Indictable Conspiracies at Common Law", Amer. Law Rev. (Jan.-Feb., 1887) Vol. XXI. Pp. 41-69.

Dorman. L. M., "The Boycott and its Methods", Criminal Law Mag. (Jan., 1887) Vol. IX. Pp. 1-15.

Welford, B. R., "The Legality of Boycotting", Va. Law Jour. (Apr., 1887) Vol. XI. PP. 196-202.

Wigmore, J. H., "The Boycott and Kindred Practices as Ground for Damages", Amer. Law Rev. (July-Aug., 1887) Vol. XXI. Pp. 509-532.

1888

Selfridge, A. J., "American Law of Boycotts and Strikes as Crimes", Amer. Law Rev.(Mar.-Apr., 1888) Vol. XXII. Pp. 233-250.

1889

Cheyney, E. P., "Decisions of the Courts in Conspiracy and Boycott Cases", Political Science Quart. (June, 1889) Vol. IV. Pp. 261-278.

1891

Burnett, John, "The Boycott as an Element in Trade Disputes", Economic Jour. (Mar., 1891) Vol. I. Pp. 163-173.

1892

"Courts of Equity and Intimidation by Labor Unions", National Corporation Reporter (Oct. 8, 15, 1892) Vol. V. Pp. 99-100, 124.

Lewis, Wm. D., ed., "Injuctions to Restrain Libels and Courts of Criminal Equity", Amer. Law Reg. and Rev. (Nov., 1892) Vol XXXI. Pp. 782-797.

McMurtrie, R., "Equity Jurisdiction Applied to Crimes and Misdemeanors", Amer. Law Reg. and Rev. (Jan., 1892) Vol. XXXI. Pp. 1-17

1893

"Actionable Boycotting", Law Times (May 6, 1893) Vol. XCV. Pp. 5-6.

"Comment on Recent Decisions in Courts Relating to Labor Unions", Yale Rev. (May, 1893) Vol. II. Pp. 8-12.

Dickson, Chas. A., "Boycotting", Central Law Jour. (Sept. 1, 1893) Vol. XXXVII. Pp. 166-169.

"Federal Injunctions against Boycotts", <u>American Law Rev.</u> (May-June, 1893) Vol. XXVII. Pp. 405-410.

Gunton, Geo., "Economics of Strikes and Boycotts", <u>Social Economist</u> (May, 1893) Vol. IV. Pp. 257-266.

Lewis, WM. D., "The Courts and the Striking Railroad Employees", Ann Harbor Cases, <u>American Law Reg. and Rev.</u> (May, 1893) Vol. XXXII. PP. 481-489.

Mason, N. T., "Organized Labor and the Law", <u>American Jour. of Politics</u> (Aug., 1893) Vol. III. Pp. 188-196.

Walker, A. F., "Recent Rulings by Federal Courts", <u>Forum</u> (May, 1893) Vol. XV. Pp. 311-322.

Aiken, Wm. P., "Legal Restraint of Strikes", <u>Yale Law Jour.</u> (Oct., 1894) Vol. IV. Pp. 13-26.

Allen, Chas. C., "Injunction and Organized Labor", <u>American Law Rev.</u> (Nov.-Dec., 1894) Vol. XXVIII. Pp. 828-859.

Bateman, Warner M., "Injunctions against Labor Unions", <u>Central Law Jour.</u> (Sept., 1894) Vol. XXXIX. Pp. 265-266.

Bullard, Herbert S., "The Injunction as a Remedy for the Boycott", <u>Yale Law Jour.</u> (June, 1894) Vol. III. Pp. 211-217.

Cogley, Thos. S., "The Law of Strikes, Lockouts, and Labor Organizations", <u>Amer. Law Rev.</u> (July-Aug., 1894) Vol. XXVIII. Pp. 629-638.

"The Debs Case", <u>Nation</u> (Sept. 13, 1894) Vol. LIX. Pp. 190-191.

"Enjoining a Threatened Railroad Strike", <u>American Law Rev.</u> (Mar.-Apr., 1894) Vol. XXVIII. Pp. 269-272.

Gregory, S. S., "The Debs Case", <u>Chicago Legal News</u> (Nov. 3, 1894) Vol. XXVII. Pp. 82.

"The Law of Stikes", <u>American Law Rev.</u> (July-Aug., 1894) Vol. XXVIII. Pp. 587, 591.

Lewis, Wm. D., "Injunction to Keep Men at Work", <u>American Law Reg. and Rev.</u> (Jan., 1894) Vol. XXXIII. Pp. 81-82 .

Lewis, Wm. D., "A Protest against Administering Criminal Law by Injunction", The Debs Case, <u>American Law Reg. and Rev.</u> (Dec., 1894) Vol. XXXIII. Pp. 879, 893.

Pingrey, D. H., "Boycotting - Its Legal Phase", <u>Central Law Jour.</u> (May 18, 1894) Vol. XXXVIII. Pp. 427-430.

1894

Reed, Chester A., "Peaceable Boycotting", Annals of Amer. Acad. of Pol. and Soc. Science (July, 1894) Vol. V. Pp. 28-47.

Selover, Geo. H., "Boycotts as Conspiracies", Minnesota Law Jour. (July, 1894) Vol. II. Pp. 167-173.

Selover, Geo. H., Economics of Boycotts", Social Economics (1894) Vol. IV. Pp. 247.

1895

Erwin, Jas. S., "Are Strikes Preventable by Judicial Action?", Criminal Law Mag. (Jan., 1895) Vol. XVII. Pp. 1-10.

"Government by Injunction", (Note) American Law Rev. (Mar.-Apr., 1895) Vol. XXIX. P. 282.

Philips, John F., "Strikes and Injunctions", American Lawyer (1895) Vol. III. P. 18.

Stanton, Stephen B., "The Mandamus as a Means of Settling Strikes", American Law Reg. and Rev. (Feb., 1895) Vol. XXXIV. Pp. 102-119.

Stimson, F. J., "The Modern Use of Injunctions", Political Science Quart. (June, 1895) Vol. X. Pp. 189-202. Also repro. in: Senate Doc. No. 190, 57th Congress, Ist Session. Pp. 114-121.

Upson, William H., "Injunctions and Strikes", Bibliotheca Sacra (July, 1895) Vol. LII. Pp. 549-552.

1896

"Government by Injunction", Gunton's Mag. (Oct., 1896) Vol. XI. Pp. 242-248.

"Injunctions-Strikes-Hamilton Brown Shoe Co. v. Saxey et al.", (Supreme Court of Missouri, Div. No. 1, Nov. 26, 1895-Annotated Case) in Central Law Jour. (Jan, 1896) Vol. XLII. Pp. 74-78.

"Injunction-Conspiracy to Injure Business-Vegelan v. Gunter", (Supreme Judicial Court of Massachusetts, Oct. 27, 1896, annotated case) in Central Law Jour. (Dec., 1896) Vol. XLII. Pp. 464-466.

Leonard, Curtis E., "Labor Riots and the So-Called 'Government by Injunction'", Engineering Mag. (Dec., 1896) Vol. XII. Pp. 381-394.

Lorimer, J. C., "Trade Union-Freedom of Contract - Malice - Picketing", Juridical Rev. (1896) Vol. VIII. Pp. 319-321. Also reprint in American Law Rev. (Sept.-Oct., 1896) Vol. XXX. Pp. 763-765.

"Picketing Injunctions against Strikes", Harvard Law Rev. (Dec., 1896) Vol. X. P. 301.

Woolen, Evans, "Labor and the Injunction", Yale Rev. (May, 1896) Vol. V. Pp. 39-50.

1896

Yarros, Victor, "Labor's Rights in the Courts", American Federationist (Nov., 1896) Vol. III. Pp. 181-183.

1897

"Answers from Eminent Jurists and Laymen to Questions on Injunctions in Labor Disputes", Chicago Times Herald (Sept. 19, 1897) Vol. XXXIV. Pp. 25-28.

Barker, Wharton, "Are the Rights of Capital Superior to the Rights of Man?", American(Philadelphia) (Aug. 21, 1897) Vol. XXVII. Pp. 117-119.

Dean, Ben S., "Government by Injunction", Green Bag (Dec., 1897) Vol. IX. Pp. 540-544.

"Federal Injunctions against Strikes and Lockouts in West Virginia", American Law Rev. (Sept.-Oct., 1897) Vol. XXXI. Pp. 761-764.

Gompers, Samuel, "Government by Injunction", American Federationist (June 1897) Vol. IV. P. 82.

Gompers, Samuel, "Injunctions Unrespected", American Federationist (Sept., 1897) Vol. IV. Pp. 159-160.

"Government by Injunction in America", Saturday Rev. (Sept. 25, 1897) Vol. LXXXIV. P. 335.

Hargis, Thomas F., "Government bu Injunction", American Federationist (Dec., 1897) Vol. IV. Pp. 227-228.

"Labor Combinations and the Law", Albany Law Jour. (April 17, 1897) Vol. LV. Pp. 250-251.

Peterkin, W. G., "Government by Injunction", Virginia Law Reg. (Dec., 1897) Vol. III. Pp. 549-563.

"Power of the U. S. Courts to Enjoin Persons fron Obstructing Interstate Commerce and Transportation of the Mails", Chicago Legal News. (Aug. 28, Sept. 4, 11, 18, 25, and Oct. 2, 1897) Vol. XXX. Pp. 2-3, 13-14, 27, 34, 39-40, 46-47.

Sedgwick, A. G., "An Injunction Sumposium", Nation (Sept. 30, 1897) Vol. LXV. Pp. 256-257.

Sedgwick, A. G., "The Strike Injunction". Nation (Aug. 26, 1897) Vol. LXV. Pp. 160-161.

1898

Edwards, P. L., "Government by Injunction", Albany Law Jour. (Jan., 1898) Vol. LVII. Pp. 8-12.

Freund, Ernst, "Justice and Unlawful Interference", Harvard Law Rev. (Feb. 25, 1898) Vol. XI. (7): Pp. 449-465.

1898

Gregory, C. N., "Government by Injunction", <u>Harvard Law Rev.</u> (Mar., 1898) Vol. XI. Pp. 487-511.

"Injunctions against Boycotting", <u>American Law Rev.</u> (Jan.-Feb., 1898) Vol. XXXII. Pp. 124-127.

"Injunctions against Boycotting", <u>American Law Rev.</u> (Jan.-Feb., 1898) Vol. XXXII. Pp. 117-119.

"The Injunction against the Striking Laborers of the American Steel and Wire Co.", <u>American Law Rev.</u> (Nov.-Dec., 1898) Vol. XXXII. Pp. 894-896.

Krauthoff, L. C., "Malice as an Ingredient in Boycott Actions", <u>American Bar Association Reports</u> (1898)

Lewis, Wm. D., "Strikes and Courts of Equity", <u>American Law Reg.</u> (Jan., 1898) Vol. XLVI. Pp. 1-12.

Patteson, S. S., "Government by Injunction", <u>Virginia Law Reg.</u> (Jan., 1898) Vol. III. Pp. 625-635.

Peterkin, W. G., "Government by Injunction", <u>American Lawyer</u> (Jan., 1898) Vol. Vi. Pp. 5-8.

Stillman, Jas. W., "The Misuses of Injunction", <u>Arena</u> (Aug., 1898) Vol. XX. Pp. 194-206.

Stimson, F. J., "The True Attitude of Courts and Legislatures upon Labor Questions", <u>Green Bag</u> (Mar., 1898) Vol. X. Pp. 103-107.

1899

Cheyney, E. P., "Decisions of the Courts in Conspiracy and Boycott Cases", <u>Political Science Quart.</u> (June, 1899) Vol. IV. Pp. 261-278.

Gompers, Samuel, "The Boycotts as a Legitimate Weapon", <u>American Federationist</u> (Oct., 1899) Vol. VI. Pp. 192-195.

Thompson, Seumour D., "Injunction against Boycotting", <u>American Law Rev.</u> (Nov.-Dec., 1899, April, 1900) Vol. XXXIII. Pp. 885-888. Vol. XXXIV. Pp. 161-185.

Yarros, Victor, "Labor and Government by Injunction", <u>American Federationist</u> (Feb., 1899) Vol. V . Pp. 231-233.

1900

Bracken, Frances B., "Trade Organizations for Collecting of Debts Due to Members by Means of the Boycott", <u>American Law Reg.</u>(Philadelphia 1900) Vol. XLVIII. (N.O. Vol. XXXIX). Pp. 691-716.

1900

Gompers, Samuel, "The Right of Picketing", American Federationist
(Mar., 1900) Vol. VII. Pp. 68-69.

Gompers, Samuel, "The Right of Picketing", American Federationist
(may, 1900) Vol. VII. Pp. 136-147.

Gompers, Samuel, "Judge Freeman's Notorious Injunction", American
Federationist (June, 1900) Vol. VII. Pp. 162-164.

Gompers, Samuel, "Editorial on Injunctions", American Federationist
(July, 1900) Vol. VII. Pp. 212-214.

Gompers, Samuel, "English Hostilities to Injunctions", American
Federationist (Nov., 1900) Vol. VII. Pp. 350-351.

Gompers, Samuel, "Government by Injunction Defined", Outlook (June,
1900) Vol. LXV. P. 231.

Miller, J. A., "Government by Injunction", Nation (Sept., 1900)
Vol. LXXI. P. 228.

Morancy, Frank W., "Injunctions against Boycotting", American Law
Rev. (May-June, 1900) Vol. XXXIV. Pp. 468-469.

"Right of Picketing Judicially Sustained", American Federationist
(Aug., 1900) Vol. VII. Pp. 240-242.

Tandy, Francis D., "Strikes, Trusts, Boycotts and Blacklists", Arena
(Feb., 1900) Vol. XXIII. Pp. 194-203.

Thompson, Seymour D., "Injunctions against Boycotting", American Law
Rev. (Mar.-Apr., 1900) Vol. XXXIV. Pp. 161-185.

1901

Gompers, Samuel, "Conflicting Decisions on Labor's Rights", American
Federationist (Mar., 1901) Vol. VIII. Pp. 80-82.

Gompers, Samuel, "Injunctions to Prevent Strikes", American Federationist (May, 1901) Vol. VIII. Pp. 164-166.

Gompers, Samuel, "More Abuse of the Injunction", American Federationist
(June, 1901) Vol. VIII. Pp. 216-218.

Gompers Samuel, "The Right of 'Persuasion'", American Federationist
(Nov., 1901) Vol. VIII. Pp. 474-475.

Gompers, Samuel, "Rights Achieved Must be Maintained", American
Federationist (Sept., 1901) Vol. VIII. Pp. 359-360.

McQuinston, F. B., "Strike Breakers", Independent (Oct. 17, 1901)
Vol. LIII. P. 2457.

1902

Cooke, Frederick H., "Solidarity of Interest as Basis of Legality of Boycotting ", <u>Yale Law Jour</u>. (1902) Vol. XI., (3): Pp. 153-158.

Flower, B. O., "Promoting of Anarchy and Social Disorders", <u>Arena</u> (Oct., 1902) Vol. XXVIII. Pp. 424-428.

Gompers, Samuel, "The A.F. of L. And the Boycott", <u>American Federationist</u> (Nov., 1902) Vol. IX. Pp. 808-810.

Gompers, Samuel, "An 'Anti' Changed to a 'Pro' Injunction Bill", <u>American Federationist</u> (July, 1902) Vol. IX. Pp. 370-372.

Gompers, Samuel, "Anti-Injunction Legislation", <u>American Federationist</u> (April, 1902) Vol. IX. Pp. 180-181.

Gompers, Samuel, "Conflicting Judicial Decisions", <u>American Federationist</u> (May, 1902) Vol. IX. Pp. 234-236.

Gompers, Samuel, "Injunctions Can't Restrain Free Speech", <u>American Federationist</u> (June, 1902) Vol. IX. Pp. 299-301.

Gompers, Samuel, "A Worthy Judicial Exception", <u>American Federationist</u> (Mar., 1902) Vol. IX. Pp. 123-124.

"The Misuse of Injunction", <u>Gunton's Mag</u>. (Sept. 1902) Vol. XXIII. Pp. 226-233.

Post, Louis E., "The Abuse of Injunctions", <u>American Federationist</u> (Oct., 1902) Vol. IX. Pp. 685-687.

"Protest against Injunction Abuse", <u>American Federationist</u> (June, 1902) Vol. IX. Pp. 305-306.

Williams, F. C., "Conspiracy", <u>Lippincott's Mag</u>. (May, 1902) Vol. LXIX. Pp. 600-610.

1903

"Boycott - A Boomerang", <u>Charities and Commons</u> (Jan. 4, 1903) Vol. XIX. Pp. 1372-1373.

"Counter Injunctions against Employers in Omaha", <u>Outlook</u> (May 23, 1903) Vol. LXXIV. Pp. 199-200.

Crosley, E. H., "Abuses of Injunction", <u>Arena</u> (July, 1903) Vol. XXX. Pp. 48-51.

"Danbury Boycott", <u>Outlook</u> (Sept. 26, 1903) Vol. LXXV. Pp. 191-193.

Davenport, Daniel, "The Anti-Boycott Movement", <u>Iron Age</u> (July 16, 1903) Vol. LXXII. P. 2.

Davenport, Daniel, "The Boycott and How It Can Be Destroyed",
Iron Age (July 23, 1903) Vol. LXXII. Pp. 54-55.

Gompers, Samuel, "New Judicial Usurpation Through Injunctions",
American Federationist (May, 1903) Vol. X. Pp. 362-364.

Gompers, Samuel, "Editorial Defense of Boycotting", American
Federationist (Oct., 1903) Vol. X. Pp. 1038-1039.

Gompers, Samuel, "Some More Judge Made Laws", American Federationist ()ct., 1903) Vol. X. Pp. 1039-1042.

Haldane, R. B., "The Laborer and the Law", Contemporary Rev.
(Mar., 1903) Vol. XXXIII. Pp. 362-372.

Hendrick, B. J., "Boycotting Battle against the Sherman Law",
McClure's Mag. (Oct., 1903) Vol. XXXI. Pp. 665-680.

"Ignoring of Boycotts", Cassier's Mag. (Feb., 1903) Vol. XXIII.
Pp. 577-578.

"Labor Injunctions", Gunton's Mag. (Apr., 1903) Vol. XXIV.
Pp. 348-351.

McClennen, Edward F., "Some of the Rights of Traders and Laborers",
Harvard Law Rev. (Feb., 1903) Vol. XVI. (4): Pp. 237-254.

Miller, James A., "The Courts on Organized Labor", Iron Age
(Mar. 5, 1903) Vol. LXXI. Pp. 19-22.

"Recent Decisions against Intimidation", American Law Rev.
(Jan.-Feb., 1903) Vol. XXXVII. Pp. 148-149.

"Recent Decisions Enjoining Persuading Railway Employees to Strike",
American Law Rev. (Mar.-Apr., 1903) Vol. XXXVI. Pp. 285-289.

"Recent Decisions against Persuading Railway Employees to Strike",
American Law Rev. (May-June, 1903) Vol. XXXVII. Pp. 461-462.

"Recent Decisions-Injunctions to Protect Labor Unions", American
Law Rev. (Nov.-Dec., 1903) Vol. XXXVII. Pp. 932-934.

Seabury, S., "Abuses of Injunction", Arena (June, 1903) Vol. XXIX.
Pp. 561-567.

Steffee, John G., "The Taff Vals Case", American Law Rev. (May-
June, 1903) Vol. XXXVII. Pp. 385-394.

"Wabash Railroad Case", Outlook (Mar. 14, 1903) Vol. LXXIII.
Pp. 599-600.

"Wabash Railroad Case", Outlook (April 11, 1903) Vol. LXXIII.
Pp. 843.

"The Waterbury Injunction", <u>Gunton's Mag.</u> (Apr., 1903) Vol. XXIV.
Pp. 283-286.

White, Henry, "Remedies for the Boycott", <u>Nation</u> (Mar. 19, 1903)
Vol. LXXVI. Pp. 222-223.

Wyman, Bruce, "The Law as to the Boycott", <u>Green Bag</u> (May, 1903)
Vol. XV. Pp. 208-215.

1904

Bayne, Howard R., "To Prevent Injunctions in Trade Union Disputes",
<u>Railroad Gazette</u> (March, 1904) Vol. XXXVI. Pp. 212-213.

"Boycotting, Injunctions, Strikes", <u>American Architect</u> (International)
(Aug. 27, 1904) Vol. LXXXV. Pp. 70-71.

Darling, Chas. R., "The Law of Strikes and Boycotts", <u>American Law
Reg.</u> (Feb., 1904) Vol. LII. Pp. 73-117.

Furuseth, A., "The Essence of Injunctions", <u>American Federationist</u>
(May, 1904) Vol. XI. Pp. 386-391.

"Gompers' Argument on the Anti-Injunction Bill", <u>American Federa-
tionist</u> (Apr., 1904) Vol. XI. Pp. 309-312.

Gompers, Samuel, "The Injunction Mania", <u>American Federationist</u>
(May, 1904) Vol. XI. Pp. 397-399.

Gompers, Samuel, "Invading Labor's Rights", <u>American Federationist</u>
(Feb., 1904) Vol. XI. Pp. 129-130.

Gompers, Samuel, "Misrepresenting the Anti-Injunction Bill",
<u>American Federationist</u> (Mar., 1904) Vol. XI. Pp. 218-220.

Livernash, Edw. J., "Why Injunctions Should not Apply", <u>American
Federationist</u> (July, 1904) Vol. XI. P. 602.

"Restraining Injunctions", <u>Gunton's Mag.</u> (April, 1904) Vol. XXVI.
Pp. 291-299.

Rooker, Wm. V., "A Thesis on Injunctions", <u>American Federationist</u>
(May, 1904) Vol. XI. Pp. 381-385.

Torrey, Jas. H., "Labor and the Law", <u>American Federationist</u>
(Oct., 1904) Vol. XII. Pp. 427-430.

1905

Ames, Jas. B., "How Far an Act May be a Tort Because of the
Wrongful Motive", <u>Harvard Law Rev.</u> (1905) Vol. XVIII. Pp. 411-422.

Beveridge, W. H., "The Reform of Union Labor Law", <u>Economic Rev.</u>
(Apr., 1905) Vol. XV. Pp. 129-149.

1905

Clark, L. D., "The Present Legal Status of Organized Labor in the United States", Jour. of Political Economy (March, 1905) Vol. XIII. Pp. 173-200.

Edwards, P. L., "Labor Strikes and Injunctions", Albany Law Jour. (July, 1905) Vol. LXVII. Pp. 209-214. Also, Central Law Jour. (July 8, 1905) Vol. LIX. Pp. 23-28.

Gompers, Samuel, "A Just Court Decision", American Federationist (Feb., 1905) Vol. XII. Pp. 76-78.

Gompers, Samuel, "Some Notions on Injunction Legislation", American Federationist (Mar., 1905) Vol. XII. Pp. 141-144.

Gompers, Samuel, "Jenkins on Injunctions and Strikes", American Federationist (July, 1905) Vol. XII. Pp. 443-445.

Gompers, Samuel, "No Property Right in Labor", American Federationist (Nov., 1905) Vol. XII. Pp. 835-836.

Huffcut, E. W., "Interference with Contracts and Business in New York", Harvard Law Rev. (1905) Vol. XVIII. Pp. 423-443.

Lewis, W. D., "The Closed Market, The Union Shop and the Common Law", Harvard Law Rev. (1905) Vol. XVIII. Pp. 444-451.

Marcosson, I. F., "The Fight for the Open Shop", World's Work (Dec., 1905) Vol. XI. Pp. 6955-6965.

"Tempering 'Government by Injunction'", Literary Digest (Feb. 18, 1905) Vol. XXX. Pp. 232-233.

1906

"Anti-Injunction Agitation", Charities and Commons (Apr. 7, 1906) Vol. XVI. Pp. 84-85.

Bryan, Jas. W., "Injunctions against Boycotts and Similar Unlawful Acts", Amer. Law Rev. (Mar.-Apr., 1906) Vol. XL. Pp. 196-211.

Bryan, Jas. W., "Injunction against Strikes", American Law Rev. (Jan.-Feb., 1906) Vol. XL. Pp. 47-50.

Freund, Ernst, "Recent Ill. Decisions Regarding Injunctions in the Course of Strikes", Jour. of Political Economy (Jan., 1906) Vol. XIV. Pp. 43-46.

Furuseth, Andrew, "No Property Rights in Man", American Federationist (May, 1906) Vol. XIII. Pp. 310-316.

Gompers, Samuel, "Developments in the Injunction Fight", American Federationist (Feb., 1906) Vol. XIII. Pp. 89-92.

Gompers, Samuel, "A Fair Injunction Decision", American Federationist (Oct., 1906) Vol. XIII. Pp. 816-818.

Gompers, Samuel, "The Injunction in Labor Disputes Must Go", American Federationist (Apr., 1906) Vol. XIII. Pp. 228-230.

Gompers, Samuel, "Injunctions Extended - Where Next?", American Federationist (July, 1906) Vol. XIII. Pp. 467-469.

Gompers, Samuel, "Judge Holdom's Injunction Frenzy", American Federationist (Mar., 1906) Vol. XIII. Pp. 156-158.

Gompers, Samuel, "Labor Legislation Here and in England", American Federationist (May, 1906) Vol. XIII. Pp. 320-322.

Gompers, Samuel, "A Letter to President T. Roosevelt", American Federationist (June, 1906) Vol. XIII. Pp. 377-380.

Gompers, Samuel, "Two Courts on Picketing", American Federationist (Jan., 1906) Vol. XIII. Pp. 28-31.

Grant, L. "Effects of Labor Injunctions", Times Mag. (Dec., 1906) Vol. I. Pp. 68-72.

"Boycott by Labor Declared to be Illegal", American Industries (Dec. 15, 1907) Vol. VI. Pp. 22-23.

"Conspiracy-Labor Unions", Central Law Jour. (Oct. 4, 1907) Vol. LXV. Pp. 258-261.

Donnell, F. G., "Injunctions against Strikes-Boycotts-and Similar Unlawful Acts", Central Law Jour. (Oct. 11, 1907) Vol. LXV. P. 273.

Gompers, Samuel, "Congressional Juggling and Sophistry with the Injunction Issue", American Federationist (Apr., 1907) Vol. XIV. Pp. 256-258.

Gompers, Samuel, "Federal Injunctions Jolted", American Federationist (Oct., 1907) Vol. XIV. Pp. 790-791.

Gompers, Samuel, "Judicial Perversion of Law against Labor", American Federationist (Jan., 1907) Vol. XIV., Pp. 36-38.

Gompers, Samuel, "Is the Boycott un-American?", American Federationist (Nov., 1907) Vol. XIV. Pp. 875-880.

Gompers, Samuel, "Taft, The Injunction Candidate", American Federationist ((Nov., 1907) Vol. XIV. Pp. 872-873.

Gompers, Samuel, "Van Cleave Seeks an Injunction against A.F. of L.", American Federationist (Oct., 1907) Vol. XIV. Pp. 784-785.

1907

Huebner, G. F., "Definitions-Laws and Judicial Decisions Regarding Boycotts", <u>Government</u> (June, 1907) Vol. I. Pp. 36-37.

Judson, F. N., "The Labor Decisions of Judge Taft", <u>Rev. of Reviews</u> (Aug., 1907) Vol. XXXIV. Pp. 212-214.

Kennedy, J. C., "Socialistic Tendencies in American Trade Unions", <u>Jour. of Political Economy</u> (1907) Vol. XV. Pp. 470-488.

"Labor's Attitude Towards the Writ of Injunction", <u>Charities and Commons</u> (Nov. 2, 1907) Vol. XIX. P. 1016.

"Labor Unions as Monopolies Imposing Illegal Restraint Upon Trade and Commerce", <u>Central Law Jour.</u> (Oct. 4, 1907) Vol. LXV. Pp. 261-262.

Littlefield, Chas. E., "Most Revolutionary of all Class Labor Propositions", <u>American Industries</u> (Jan. 1, 1907) Vol. V. Pp. 1-4.

McWilliams, R. L., "Evolution of Law Relating to Boycotts", <u>Amer. Law Rev.</u> (May-June, 1907) Vol. XLI. Pp. 336-342.

McWilliams, R. L., "Labor Litigation-Strikes and Boycotts", <u>Amer. Law Rev.</u> (May-June, 1907) Vol. XLI. Pp. 448-451.

Meier, W. F., "The Attitude of Equity Towards th eStrikes and Boycott- The Use of the Injunction", <u>Law Notes</u> (May, 1907) Vol. XI. Pp. 27-31.

Otis, H. G., "'Long Winning Fight by the Los Angeles Times Against the Closed Shop", <u>World's Work</u> (Dec., 1907) Vol. XV. Pp. 9675-9679.

Segar, H. R., "The Legal Status of Trade Unions in the United Kingdom with Conclusions Applicable to the United States", <u>Political Science Quart.</u> (Dec., 1907) Vol. XXII. Pp. 611-629.

Smith, Jeremiah, "Crucial Issues inLabor Litigation", <u>Harvard Law Rev.</u> (Feb.-Apr., 1907) Vol. XX. Pp. 253-279, 345-362, 429-455.

Spelling, T. C., "The Point of Injunction", <u>American Federationist</u> (June, 1907) Vol. XIV. Pp. 401-407.

Van Cleave, Jas. W., "The Boycott and the Blacklist", <u>American Industries</u> (Oct. 15, 1907) Vol. VII. Pp. 12-14.

1908

Alger, Geo. W., "Taft and Labor", <u>McClures Mag.</u> (Sept., 1908) Vol. XXXI. Pp. 597-602.

"Amend the Sherman Anti-Trust Law- Labor must Exercise its Political Power", <u>American Federationist</u> (May, 1908) Vol. XV. Pp. 354-364.

"The Anti-Trust Act and the Boycott", <u>Legal Intelligence</u> (1908) Vol. XX. Pp. 34-35.

Baldwin, E. F., "Government by Injunction", American Federationist (Nov., 1908) Vol. XV. Pp. 953-955.

Beck, James, M., "Injunction in Labor Cases. Arguments Before Senate Judiciary Committee", American Industries (Feb. 15, 1908) Vol. VII. P. 20.

"Boycott Illegal", Outlook (Feb. 15, 1908) Vol. LXXXVIII. Pp. 342-343.

"The Boycott Perpetually Enjoined. Justice Clabaugh's Decision", American Industries (Apr. 1, 1908) Vol. VII. P. 17.

"Boycott as Restraint of Trade Combinations under the Anti-Trust Law", Yale Law Jour. (June, 1908) Vol. XVII. Pp. 616-618.

"Boycott Unlawful", Independent (Feb. 13, 1908) Vol. LXIV. Pp. 381-382.

"Boycotting Interstate Commerce, Case of Loewe v. Lawlor", Case and Comment (Apr., 1908) Vol. XIV. Pp. 154-155.

Burdick, Francis, M.,"Injunctions in Labor Disputes", North American Rev. (Aug., 1908) Vol. CLXXXVIII. Pp. 273-284.

Chandler, William E., "The Labor Union, the Injunction and the Trust", Collier's Mag. (Oct. 10, 1908) Vol. XLIV. P.24.

"Concerning Injunctions", Outlook (Aug., 1908) Vol. LXXXIX. Pp. 786-789.

Darling, Charles R., "Recent Decisions in America and English Legislation Affecting Labor", Amer. Law Rev. (Mar.-Apr., 1908) Vol. XLII. Pp. 200-228.

Dwight, Frederick, "The Origin and Use of Injunction", Independent (Aug. 13, 1908) Vol. LXV. Pp. 348-351.

Emery, James A., "The Truth about Injunctions", American Industries (July 15, 1908) Vol. VII. Pp. 25-26.

Gompers, Samuel, "The Abuse of Injunctions", Independent (Aug. 27, 1908) Vol. LXV. Pp. 460-463.

Gompers, Samuel, "Amendment to the Sherman Anti-Trust Law", American Federationist (July, 1908) Vol. XV. Pp. 538-541.

Gompers, Samuel, "Both Parties have Spoken - Choose Between Them", American Federationist (Aug., 1908) Vol. XV. Pp. 598-606.

Gompers, Samuel, "The Cry for More (in) Equity", American Federationist (Sept., 1908) Vol. XV. Pp. 740-743.

Gompers, Samuel, "The Essence of Labor's Contention on Injunction", American Federationist (Aug., 1908) Vol. XV. pp. 611-613.

Gompsers, Samuel, "Free Press and Free Speech Invaded by Injunction against A.F. of L.", *American Federationist* (Feb., 1908) Vol. XV. Pp. 98-105.

Gompers, Samuel, "Injunction Contempt Proceeding", *American Federationist* (Oct., 1908) Vol. XV. Pp. 852-858.

Gompers, Samuel, "Judge Upholds Labor's Injunction Contention", *American Federationist* (July, 1908) Vol. XV. Pp. 529-531.

Gompers, Samuel, "Labor Organizations Must not be Outlawed - the Supreme Court's Dicision in the Hatters' Case", *American Federationist* (Mar., 1908) Vol. XV. Pp. 180-192.

Gompers, Samuel, "Labor and the Anti-Trust Law", *American Federationist* (May, 1908) Vol. XV. Pp. 366-388.

Gompers, Samuel, "President T. Roosevelt's Attack on Labor Answered", *American Federationist* (Nov., 1908) Vol. XV. Pp. 973-980.

Gould, Ashley M., "Order Granting Injunction. Buck's Stove and Range Co. v. Amer. Fed. of Labor", *American Federationist* (Feb., 1908) Vol. XV. Pp. 114-115.

Groat, George Gorham, "The Courts' Views of Injunctions in Labor Disputes", *Political Science Quart.* (Sept., 1908) Vol. XXIII. Pp. 408-439.

Hendrick, Burton J., "The Battle against the Sherman Law. How Capital and Labor Combine to Safeguard the Trust and Legalize the Boycott", *McClure's Mag.* (Oct., 1908) Vol. XXXI. Pp. 665-680.

Hourwich, Isaac A., "Injunctions", *Moody's Mag.* (Oct., 1908) Vol. VI. Pp. 270-273.

"Illegitimate Injunctions", *Outlook* (May 22, 1908) Vol. LXXXIX. Pp. 132-133.

"Injunctions", *Exponent* (St. Louis) (Mar., 1908) Vol. V. Pp. 13-14.

"Injunctions against Boycotts", *Charities and Commons* (Mar., 1908) Vol. XIX. P. 1718.

"Injunction - Controversy and Boycott", *Current Literature* (July, 1908) Vol. XLV. Pp. 6-8.

"Intolerable Tyranny. Street Railroad Strike in Chester, Pa.", *Outlook* Vol. LXXXIX. Pp. 134-135.

"Justice Gould's Decision - The Boycott", *American Industries* (Jan. 1, 1908) Vol. VI. Pp. 5-9.

"Justice Gould's Decision on the Boycott", *Albany Law Jour.* (Jan., 1908) Vol. LXX. Pp. 8-13.

Kennedy, John C., "An Important Labor Injunction", Jour. of Political Economy (Feb., 1908) Vol. XVI. Pp. 102-105.

"Labor Leaders and the Supreme Court", Current Literature (May, 1908) Vol. XLIV. Pp. 468-472.

"Labor Leaders Sentenced - Boycott of Buck's Stove and Range Co. of St. Louis", Independent (Dec. 31, 1908) Vol. LXV. Pp. 1585-1586.

"Supreme Court Decisions in the Hatters' Case - Affects All Organized Labor", American Federationist (Mar., 1908) Vol. XV. Pp. 161-178.

"Labor Organizations Must not be Outlawed", American Federationist (Mar., 1908) Vol. XV. Pp. 180-192.

"Labor Organizations in Legislation", Michigan Law Rev. (June, 1908) Vol. VI. Pp. 609-623.

"Labor's Responsibility in the Boycott", American Industries (Jan., 1908) Vol. VI. Pp. 5-6.

Lewis, Henry Harrison, "The Peril of Anti-Injunction Legislation", North American Rev. (Oct., 1908) Vol. CLXXXVIII. Pp. 577-583.

"Lindsay & Co. v. Montana Federation of Labor", Political Science Quart. (1908) Vol. XXIV. Pp. 86.

Littlefield, C. E., "Class Legislation", Exponent (St. Louis) (Apr., 1908) Vol. V. Pp. 6-9, 15.

Littlefield, C. E., "The President and the Courts", American Industries (July 1, 1908) Vol. VII. Pp. 11-14.

Low, Seth, "The Writ on Injunction as a Party Issue", Century Mag. (Oct., 1908) Vol. LXXVI. Pp. 911-916.

Mahon, John, "Labor and the Judiciary", Amer. Law Rev. (July-Aug., 1908) Vol. XLII. Pp. 598-601.

"Mine Workers on Injunctions. Resolutions Adopted by the 'United Mine Workers of America'", American Federationist (July, 1908) Vol. XV. Pp. 542-543.

Trickett, W., "The Rationale of the Injunction", Amer. Law Rev. (Sept.-Oct., 1908) Vol. XLII. Pp. 687-705.

Silverstein, David, "Injunctions in Labor Cases", American Federationist (July, 1908) Vol. XV. Pp. 517-519.

Speer, William H., "Anti-Injunction Legislation", American Industries (June 1, 1908) Vol. VII. Pp. 12-13.

Stevens, F. W., "Proper Use of the Writ of Injunction from the Stand-point of Legal History", Columbia Law Rev. (Nov., 1908) Vol. VIII. Pp. 561-566.

Trieber, Jacob, "Injunctions and the Judiciary", Independent (Aug., 1908) Vol. LXV. Pp. 352-354.

Turner, George Kibbee, "What Organized Labor Wants", American Federationist (Dec., 1908) Vol. XV. Pp. 1057-1063. Also, McClure's Mag. (Nov., 1908) Vol. XXXII. Pp. 25-31.

Van Cleave, Jas. W., "The Doom of the Boycott", American Industries (Feb., 1908) Vol. VII. Pp. 16.

White, Henry, "The Labor Unions in the Presidential Campaign". North American Rev. (Sept., 1908) Vol. CLXXXVIII. Pp. 372-382.

"Amending the Sherman Anti-Trust Law", National Civic Federation Rev. (Mar., 1909) Vol. III. Pp. 14-15.

Bope, George W., "Wrongs to be Righted", American Federationist (July, 1909) Vol. XVI. Pp. 593-596.

"The Boycott and Free Speech", Outlook (Nov. 13-20, 1909) Vol. XCIII. Pp. 562, 604-608.

Boyle, James, "Organized Labor and Cpurt Decisions", Forum (Dec., 1909) Vol. XLII. Pp. 535-551.

"Boycott Decision against Milwaukee Papers", Chautauquian (Jan., 1909) Vol. XL. Pp. 409-410.

"Civic Federation on Black and White Lists", Survey (Apr. 10, 1909) Vol. XXII. Pp. 88-89.

"Contempt Decision of Justice Wright", American Industries (Jan. 1, 1909) Vol. VIII. Pp. 8-18.

"Contempt of Samuel Gompers", Current Literature (Feb., 1909) Vol. XLVI. Pp. 124-132.

"Conviction of Labor Leaders", Outlook (Jan. 2, 1909) Vol. XCI. Pp. 3-6.

Cook, E. Wake, "King Boycott- A New Potentate", East and West (Jan., 1909) Vol. VIII. Pp. 53-56.

"Courts of Appeals of the District of Columbia", American Federationist (Dec., 1909) Vol. XVI. Pp. 1037-1059.

"Court of Appeals, D.C., American Federation v. Buck's Stove and Range Co.", American Federationist (Apr., 1909) Vol. XVI. Pp. 313-335.

"Court of appeals, D.C. No. 1916. Decided Mar. 11, 1909". Chicago Legal News (Mar. 20, 1909) Vol. XLI. Pp. 265-268, 270-272.

Drew, Walter, "A Legal Decision of the Boycott", Square Deal (Sept., 1909) Vol. V. Pp. 100-108.

"Enjoining Argument by Persuasion". Central Law Rev. (Oct. 29, 1909) Vol. LXIX. Pp. 315-316.

"Famous Boycott Case", American Rev. of Reviews, (Feb., 1909) Vol. XXXIX. Pp. 145-146.

Fauntleroy, Cornelius H., "Government by Injunction", Central Law Jour. (Aug. 29, 1909) Vol. LXIX. Pp. 129-135.

Gompers, Samuel, "Buck's Stove and Range Co. - Injunction Modified", American Federationist (April, 1909) Vol. XVI. Pp. 336-343.

Gompers, Samuel, "Comment on Justice Wright's Decision", American Federationist (Mar., 1909) Vol. XVI. Pp. 216-229.

Gompers, Samuel, "Justice Wright's Decision in Gompers, Mitchell and Morrison Case", American Federationist (Feb., 1909) Vol. XVI. Pp. 438-456.

Gompers Samuel, "Justice Wright's Denial of Free Speech and Free Press", American Federationist (Feb., 1909) Vol. XVI. Pp. 130-132.

Gompers, Samuel, "President T. Roosevelt's Message on Labor", American Federationist (Jan., 1909) Vol. XVI. Pp. 40-47.

"The Gompers, Mitchell and Morrison Sentence Affirmed", Square Deal (Dec., 1909) Vol. V. Pp. 389-434.

Hale, Richard W., "Injunctions and Pardons", American Law Rev. (Mar.-Apr., 1909) Vol. XLIII. Pp. 492-504.

"History of Buck's Stove and Range Company's Boycott Case", American Industries (Jan. 1, 1909) Vol. VIII. Pp. 23-33.

"Injunction with Damages, Westchester County", New York Labor Bulletin (June, 1909) Vol. XLI. Pp. 242-246.

"Injunction Law. Boycotts and Labor Unions", National Corporation Reports (Jan. 21 and 28, 1909) Vol. XXXVII. Pp. 710-715, 746-750.

"Justice Wright's Decision in Case of Buck's Stove and Range Co.,", American Federationist (Feb., 1909) Vol. XVI. Pp. 101-128.

Kirby, John Jr., "Where Does President Taft Stand?", American Industries (Oct., 1909) Vol. X. Pp. 10-12.

Lennon, John B., "Unjust Injunctions Work for Personal Freedom", American Federationist (Aug., 1909) Vol. XVI. Pp. 671-672.

1909

Low, Seth, "The Contempt Cases of Messrs. Gompers, Mitchell and Morrison", National Civic Federation Rev. (Mar., 1909) Vol. III. P. 13.

MacDonald, Edward A., "The Right of a Trade Union to Enforce a Boycott", Michigan Law Rev. (Apr., 1909) Vol. VII. Pp. 499-502.

Martin, John, "Labor Unions and the Boycott", Charities and Commons (Mar. 6, 1909) Vol. XXI. Pp. 1046-1048.

Parker, Judge Alton B., "An Argument in Connection with Buck's Stove and Range Company's Contempt Case", American Federationist (Jan., 1909) Vol. XVI. Pp. 17-30.

"Right to Restrain the Right of Free Speech or a Free Press", Central Law Jour. (Mar. 19, 1909) Vol. LXVIII. Pp. 207-208.

Schaffner, Margaret A., "Injunctions in Labor Disputes", Charities and Commons, (Mar., 1909) Vol. XXI. P. 2136.

Speer, William A., "Recent Cabot Decisions", Exponent St. Louis (Feb., 1909) Vol. VI. Pp. 6-8.

Stote, Ames, "What the Boycott Cost the Nation", Moody's Mag. (May, 1909) Vol. VII. Pp. 370-373.

Taft, William H., "Judicial Decisions as an Issue in Politics", McClure's Mag. (June, 1909) Vol. XXXIII. Pp. 201-209.

Taylor, Graham, "From the Judges to the Lawmakers", Charities and Commons (Jan. 16, 1909) Vol. XXI. Pp. 693-694.

Thomas, David Y., "A Year of Bench Labor Law", Political Science Quart. (Mar., 1909) Vol. XXIV. Pp. 80-94.

"The Unfair List and the Freedom of the Press", Chicago Legal News (Feb. 20, 1909) Vol. XLI. P. 233.

Veeder, Van Vechter, "Absolute Immunity in Defamation - Judicial Proceedings", Columbia Law Rev. (June, 1909) Vol. IX. Pp. 463-491.

1910

Allen, A.M., "Criminal Conspiracies in Restraint of Trade at Common Law", Harvard Law Rev. (May, 1910) Vol. XXIII. Pp. 531-538.

"Administration of Justice in the United States", Annals of Amer. Acad. of Pol. and Soc. Science (Sept., 1910) Vol. XXXVI. P. 1.

Bennett, A. W., "Unions may Boycott - Decision in Oklahoma State", American Federationist (Mar., 1910) Vol. XVII. Pp. 228-230.

Bettman, Gilbert, "Contempt Procedure in Equity", American Federationist (Feb., 1910) Vol. XVII. Pp. 116-118.

Bryan, James W., "Proper Bounds for the Use of the Injunction in Labor Disputes", Annals of Amer. Acad. of Pol. and Soc. Science (Sept., 1910) Vol. XXXVI. Pp. 288-301.

Caldwell, Henry Clay, "Trial by Judge and Jury", American Federationist (May, 1910) Vol. XVII. Pp. 385-389.

"Civic Federation on Black and White Lists", Survey (April, 1910) Vol. XXII. Pp. 88-89.

Collier, M. C., "Criminal Conspiracy Needs Overt Act to make it Indictable", Century Law Jour. (Dec. 2, 1910) Vol. LXXI. Pp. 387-392.

Emery, James A., "Injunction Practically Considered", Square Deal (June, 1910) Vol. VI. Pp. 385-394.

Emery, James A., "The Administration Injunction Bill", American Industries (March, 1910) Vol. X. Pp. 28-29.

Frazier, Walter S., "Injunctions", Outlook (Oct. 1, 1910) Vol. XCVI. Pp. 288-289.

Furuseth, Andrew, " Government by Injunction-Misuse of Equity Power", Central Law Rev. (July, 1910) Vol. LXXII. Pp. 5-7.

Gompers, Samuel, "The President on Injunctions", American Federationist (Jan., 1910) Vol. XVII. Pp. 45-48.

Gompers, Samuel, "The Hatters' Case - The Sherman Law - Amend It or End It", American Federationist (Mar., 1910) Vol. XVII. Pp. 197-204.

Gompers, Samuel, "Judicial Invasion of Guaranteed Rights", American Federationist (Apr., 1910) Vol. XVII. PP. 297-301.

Gompers, Samuel, "A Protest against Legalizing the Injunction Abuse", American Federationist (April, 1910) Vol. XVII. Pp. 318-320.

Gompers, Samuel, "Injunctions-Human Rights and Property Rights Confused", American Federationist (Sept., 1910) Vol. XVII. Pp. 590-593.

Gompers, Samuel, "Buck's Stove and Range Company's Agreement with Organized Labor", American Federationist (Sept. 1910) Vol. XVII. Pp. 807-812.

Gompers, Samuel, "Free Speech and the Injunction Order", Annals of Amer. Acad. of Pol. and Soc. Science (Sept., 1910) Vol. XXXVI. No. 1. Pp. 255-264.

"Illegal Boycott- The Danbury Hatters", Outlook (Feb. 19, 1910) Vol. XCIV. Pp. 370-371.

1910

"Interference with Employers Business by Combination of Labor",
Columbia Law Rev. (Nov., 1910) Vol. X. Pp. 652-654.

Littlefield, Chas. E., "The Use and Abuse of Injunctions in Labor
Controversies", Case and Comment (Sept., 1910) Vol. XVII. Pp. 173-178.

Merritt, Walter Gordon, "The Significance of the Loewe Decision",
American Industries (Mar., Apr., May, 1910) Vol. X. Pp. 22-23, 25-27,
28-29, 46.

Merritt, Walter Gordon, "Law of the Danbury Hatters' Case", Annals of
Amer. Acad. of Pol. and Soc. Science (Sept., 1910) Vol. XXXVI.
Pp. 265-276.

Noble, H., "Sherman Anti-Trust Act and Industrial Combinations",
American Law Rev. (Mar.-Apr., 1910) Vol. XLIV. Pp. 177-199.

"Our Test Case in United States Supreme Court. Petition and Brief
in Buck's Stove and Range Co. Case", American Federationist (Jan.,
1910) Vol. XVII. Pp. 17-32.

Prim, C. J., "Labor Unions and the Anti-Trust Law, Review of Recent
Decisions", Jour. of Political Economy (Feb., 1910) Vol. XVIII.
Pp. 129-138.

Shepard, Almond G., "Boycotts - Principles Applicable in Determining
Lawfulness", Case and Comment (Sept., 1910) Vol. XVII. Pp. 159-166.
Also, American Federationist (Nov., 1910) Vol. XVII. Pp. 976-981.

Terrister, "Origin of Writ of Injunction", Central Law Rev. (Sept.,
1910) Vol. LXXI. Pp. 168-172.

"The Buck's Stove and Range Case - Proof of Conspiracy", American
Industries (Aug., 1910) Vol. XI. Pp. 5-8. Rep. Square Deal
(Sept., 1910) Vol. VII. Pp. 108-116.

"The Secondary Boycott", Outlook (Nov. 26, 1910) Vol. XCVI. P. 661.

"Union Rule or Ruin", Square Deal (Feb., 1910) Vol. VI. Pp. 38-48.

"Unions may Boycott", American Federationist (March, 1910) Vol. XVII.
P. 228.
"Use and Abuse of Injunctions", Outlook (Sept. 3, 1910) Vol. XCVI.
Pp. 14-17.

1911

"Acts Constituting Conspiracy in Commerce", Law Jour. (Jan. 28,
1911) Vol. XLVI. P. 52.

"Case of the Danbury Hatters", Outlook (Apr. 22, 1911) Vol. XCVII.
Pp. 847-849.

Edmunds, Senator George F., "The Interstate Trust and Commerce Act
of 1890", North American Rev. (Dec., 1911) Vol. CXCIV. Pp. 801.

Gompers, Samuel, "A Specimen of 'Wobbly Thinking'", American Federationist (Jan., 1911) Vol. XVIII. Pp. 29-31.

Gompers, Samuel, "The President's Habit of Mind on Injunctions", American Federationist (Jan., 1911) Vol. XVIII. Pp. 32-34.

Gompers, Samuel, "Loewe - Hatters' Case Decision Reversed", American Federationist (May, 1911) Vol. XVIII. P. 385.

Hunting, W. B., "Extra Territorial Effect of the Sherman Act", Illinois Law Rev. (May, 1911) Vol. VI. Pp. 34-35.

"Injunctions and Labor Disputes", Outlook (June 22, 1911) Vol. CI. Pp. 375-376.

Irwin, Will., "The American Newspaper", Collier's Mag. (Jan. 21 and July 29, 1911).

Joyce, H. C., "Boycotts", Century Law Jour. (April 12, 1911) Vol. LXXIV. Pp. 263-274.

Stimson, Frederick Jessup, "Law of Combined Action of Possession", American Law Rev. (Jan.-Feb., 1911) Vol. XLV. Pp. 1-24.

Walker, A. H., "Unreasonable 'Obiter Dicta' in Standard Oil Case", Century Law Jour. (June, 1911) Vol. LXXII. Pp. 413-422.

"Hatters' Case - Anti-Trust Law and Organized Labor", American Federationist (Nov., 1912)   Pp. 908.

Merritt, Walter Gordon, "The Closed Shop", North American Rev. (Jan., 1912) Vol. CXCV. Pp. 66-72.

Wigmore, J. H., "Boycott - An Action by Non-Union Employees to Enjoin a Union", Illinois Law Rev. (Dec., 1912) Vol. VII. Pp. 320-322.

Baer, M. C., "Torts - Civic Conspiracy Interference with Business", California Law Rev. (Nov., 1913) Vol. II. Pp. 85-86.

"Blacklisting Employees - May Give Record without Malice", American Employer (Dec., 1913) Pp. 301-303.

"Blow at Trade Blacklists", Literary Digest (Feb. 1, 1913) Vol. XLVI. P. 218.

Emery, James A., "Shall the Decalogue be Repealed", Square Deal (Aug., 1913) Vol.   Pp. 65-70.

"Hammond Lumber Company Anxious to Scab Eureka", Labor News (Eureka, Calif.) (Aug. 16, 1913) P. 1.

1913

"Open and Closed Shop", Review (July, 1913) Pp. 46-49.

"Right of Unions to Fight for Enforcement of Closed Shop", Columbia
Law Rev. (Jan., 1913) Vol. XIII. Pp. 66-68.

Schofield, H., "Equity Jurisdiction - Right of Workman to Enjoin
Threatened Strike", Illinois Law Rev. (June, 1913) Vol. VIII.
Pp. 126-133.

"The Boycott", Union Leader (Aug., 1913) Vol. Pp. 2-13.

"Torts - Interference with Another's Employment", Univ. of Pennsylvania Law Rev. (Feb., 1913) Vol. LXI. Pp. 255-257.

Wheeler, E.P., "What is the Matter with Injunctions", Independent
(Jan. 23, 1913) Vol. LXXIV. Pp. 196-198.

1914

"Boycott of Broker Lawful", National Corporation Reporter (May 13,
1914) Vol. L. P. 594.

"Case of the Danbury Hatters Again", Survey (Jan. 10, 1914) Vol.
XXXI. P. 429.

"Competition as a Justification of Secondary Boycott", Harvard
Law Rev. (Mar., 1914) Vol. XXVII. Pp. 478-480.

"Danbury Hatters' Case", Literary Digest (Jan. 10, 1914) Vol.
XLVIII. Pp. 53-54.

Ewing, J. N., "Boycott not Legal", Univ. of Pennsylvania Law Rev.
(Dec., 1914) Vol. LXIII. Pp. 113-115.

Gompers, Samuel, "Anti-Trust Law and Labor", American Federationist
(Jan., 1914) Vol. XXI. Pp. 35.

"Injunction in Labor Disputes", Survey (Mar. 21, 1914) Vol. XXXI.
P. 768.

Laidler, H. W., "Boycotts and the Labor Struggle", Nation (Mar. 12,
1914) VOL. XCVIII. P. 267.

Ralston, J. H. & Emery, J. A., "Injunction in Labor Disputes - for
and against", Survey (Feb. 7, 1914) Vol. XXXI. Pp. 575-582.

Seager, H. R., "Injunction", Survey (Feb. 7, 1914) Vol. XXXI.
Pp. 594-595.

Witte, Edwin E., "The Clayton Bill and Organized Labor", Survey
(1914) Vol. XXXII. P. 360.

1915

"Another Danbury Case", Law Student's Helper (May, 1915) Vol. XXIII.
Pp. 3-4.

"Contracts - Defense - Illegal Monopoly", Columbia Law Rev. (Apr.,
1915) Vol. XV. Pp. 356-357.

Davenport, Daniel, "Analysis of labor Sections of Clayton Act",
Century Law Jour. (Jan. 15, 1915) Vol. LXXX. Pp. 46-55.

H. E., "Anti-Trust Act - Combinations in Restraint of Trade", Law
Student's Helper (Mar., 1915) Vol. XXIII. Pp. 20-22.

Gregory, S. S., "Labor and the Law", American Federationist (Dec.,
1915) Vol. XXII. Pp. 1029-1039.

"Labor's Equality Before the Law", American Federationist (Mar.,
1915) Vol. XXII. Pp. 180-185.

Laidler, H. W., "Supreme Court Decision in the Danbury Hatters' Case",
Survey (Jan. 16, 1915) Vol. XXXII. Pp. 415-416.

Laidler, H. W., "The Kansas Labor Statute Case and the Supreme Court",
American Federationist (Apr., 1915) Vol. XXII. Pp. 269-271.

Megaardon, J., "The Danbury Hatters' Case" Possible Effect on Trade
Unions", American Law Rev. (May, 1915) Vol. XLIX. Pp. 417-428.

"Opinions of Eminent Subscribers on Clayton Anti-Trust Law",
American Federationist (Sept., 1915) Vol. XXII. Pp. 665-715.

"Remedy State Injunction Abuse", American Federationist (April, 1915)
Vol. XXII. Pp. 274-275.

Stowe, L. B., "Paying the Penalty in Danbury", Outlook (July 14, 1915)
Vol. CX. Pp. 612-615.

"Straight Stuff about the Danbury Hatters and Boycotting", Everybody's
Mag. (July, 1915) Vol. XXXIII. Pp. 121-123.

"The Danbury Hatters' Case", National Corporation Reports (Aug. 5,
1915) Vol. L. P. 1040.

"Union Men to Pay Boycott Damages", Literary Digest (Jan. 16, 1915)
Vol. L. Pp. 86-87.

Wickersham, Hon. George H., "Labor Legislation in the Clayton Act",
American Federationist (July, 1915) Vol. XXII. Pp. 493-503.

1916

Gompers, Samuel, "Strike 'Un' from Unfreedom", American Federationist
(Apr., 1916) Vol. XXIII. Pp. 285-287.

1916

Gompers, Samuel, "Anti-Boycotters Now Scheme in Connecticut",
American Federationist (Oct., 1916) Vol. XXIII. Pp. 960-962.

Gompers, Samuel, "Decisions of U. S. Circuit Court of Appeal – Dowd
v. Miners Case", American Federationist (Dec., 1916) Vol. XXIII.
Pp. 1149-1152.

Hamburg, A. M., "Torts – Secondary Boycotts", Cornell Law Quart.
(Jan., 1916) Vol. I.   Pp. 133-136.

1917

Gompers, Samuel, "Injunctions – a Decision – Press Forward",
American Federationist (Mar., 1917) Vol. XXIV. Pp. 2034.

Gompers, Samuel, "The Yoke Will not be Worn", American Federationist
(Feb., 1917) Vol. XXIV. Pp. 126-127.

"The Injunction Case – Paine Lumber Co.", American Federationist
(Aug., 1917) Vol. XXIV. Pp. 633-635.

Woehlke, W.V., "Boycott Loses Out", Sunset (May, 1917) Vol. XXXVIII.
Pp. 10-12.

1918

"Boycott on Materials", Harvard Law Rev. (Jan,,1918) Vol. XXXI.
Pp. 482-485.

Cook, Walter Wheeler, "Privileges of Labor Unions in the Fight for
Life", Yale Law Jour. (Apr., 1918) Vol. XXVII. Pp. 779-801.

V.E.N., "Restraint of Trade – Sherman Anti-Trust Act – Liabilities
of Unions", Univ. of Pennsylvania Law Rev.(Apr., 1918) Vol. LXVI.
Pp. 267-273.

1919

"Government by Injunction", Public (Nov. 29, 1919) Vol. XXII.
Pp. 1106-1107.

"Injunction against the Miners", New Republic (Nov. 12, 1919)
Vol. XX. Pp. 304-308.

"Strike or Boycott", Public (May 14, 1919) Vol. XXII. Pp. 509-510.

1920

"A Campaign of Social Ostracism to Promote Close Shop", Law and
Labor (Nov., 1920) Vol. II. Pp. 256-257.

"A Man May Operate His Own Moving Picture Machine", Law and Labor
(May, 1920) Vol. II. Pp. 119-120.

"Boycott by Strikes to Compel Unionization Permanently Enjoined",
Law and Labor (July, 1920) Vol. II. Pp. 178-179.

"Boycott of Common Carrier by Employees", Law and Labor (Jan., 1920)
Vol. II. Pp. 7-8.

"Federal Court Refuses to Enjoin Secondary Boycott", Law and Labor
Vol. II. Pp. 210-212.

"Federal Restraining Order against transportation Trades", Law and
Labor Vol. II. Pp. 187-188.

Fisner, Morton P., "Grounds for Issuance of Injunctions", Chicago
Legal News (July 1, 1920) Vol. LII. Pp. 386-388, 390-392.

"Injunctions as Affected by the Clayton Act", Monthly Labor Rev.
(Oct., 1920) Vol. II. Pp. 829-831.

"Interference by Combination with Freedom of Employment", Law and
Labor (Aug., 1920) Vol. II. Pp. 221-222.

"Secondary Boycotts - Clayton Act and Supreme Court", Law and Labor
Vol. II. P. 267.

"Secondary Boycott in Tranportation Trade", Law and Labor (May,
1920) Vol. II. Pp. 116-118, 167-170.

Soule, G., "Case Against the Injunction", Nation (May, 1920) Vol.
CX. Pp. 576-577.

Spargo, J., "Public in Industrial Warfare", Independent (Aug. 14,
1920) Vol. CIII. Pp. 173-176.

"Trade Unions: Injunctions and Boycotts", Virginia Law Rev. (Jan.,
1920) Vol. VI. Pp. 291-293.

"Trade Unions - Labor Litigation. Boycotts and Picketing", Minnesota
Law Rev. Vol, IV. Pp. 544-546.

"The Ohio Court Sustains Secondary Boycotts", Law and Labor (Feb.,
1920) Vol. II. Pp. 43-44.

"The Arizona Law before United States Supreme Court", Law and Labor
(May, 1920) Vol. II. Pp. 118-119.

"Action by Employees. Cited Cases", Monthly Labor Rev. (June, 1921)
Vol. XII. Pp. 1237-1239; (Apr., 1922) Vol. XIV. Pp. 818-819: (Oct.,
1922) Vol. XV. Pp. 891-897.

"Boycott - Clayton Act", Michigan Law Rev.(Apr., 1921) Vol. XIX.
Pp. 628-637. Wisconsin Law Rev.(Apr., 1921) Vol. I. Pp. 186-188;
Virginia Law Rev. (Mar., 1921) Vol. VII. Pp. 462-467.

1921

"Circulation of Union Propaganda – Not Actionable", Law and Labor (Dec., 1921) Vol. III. Pp. 286-287.

"Conspiracy to Restrain Milk Trade Enjoined", Law and Labor (Apr., 1921) Vol. III. Pp. 97-98.

"Damages Will be Awarded for Interfering with Right to Work", Law and Labor (Mar., 1921) Vol. III. Pp. 70-72.

Gompers, Samuel, "Rights Judicially Purloined", American Federationist (Feb., 1921) Vol. XXVIII. Pp. 135-136.

Gompers, Samuel, "The Courts and Mr. Taft in Labor", American Federationist (Mar., 1921) Vol. XXVIII. Pp. 220-225.

"Labor Clauses of Clayton Act before the Supreme Court", Columbia Law Rev. (Mar., 1921) Vol. XXI. Pp. 258-261.

"Labor Dred Scott Decision – Supreme Court", Literary Digest (Jan., 1921) Vol. LXVIII. Pp. 12.

"Labor Laws, Strikes, Boycotts and Picketing", California Law Rev. (Nov., 1921) Vol. X. Pp. 82-84.

"Limits to the Rights of Boycotts", Outlook (June 19, 1921) Vol. CXXVII. Pp. 83-86.

Sayre, F. B., "Clayton Act Construed in Duplex Case", Survey (Jan., 1921) Vol. XLV. Pp. 597-598.

"Secondary Boycott Boomerangs in Closed Shop", Law and Labor (Apr., 1921) Vol. III. Pp. 93-94.

"Secondary Boycott Enjoined", Monthly Labor Rev. (June, 1921) Vol. XII. Pp. 1245-1246.

"Secondary Boycott and the Clayton Act", Monthly Labor Rev. (Feb., 1921) Vol. XII. Pp. 413-416.

"Strikes and Boycotts", Harvard Law Rev. (June, 1921) Vol. XXXIV. Pp. 880-888, 891.

"The Challenge Accepted, Labor Will Not be Outlawed or Enslaved", American Federationist (Apr., 1921) Vol. XXVIII. Pp. 289-301.

1922

Adler, Philip, "The Daugherty Injunction", Survey (Sept., 1922) Vol. XLVIII. P. 702.

"A Secondary Boycott of Cut Stone Enjoined", Law and Labor (Feb., 1922) Vol. IV. Pp. 33-35.

1922

Baker, Benjamin, "Daugherty's Law Sound - Error Was in Tactics", Annalist (Sept., 1922) Vol. XX. Pp. 243-244.

Bakewell, Paul, "Strike Injunction - Legal Basis", American Industries (Nov., 1922) Vol. XXIII. Pp. 9, 10, 16, 23.

"Blacklist - Secondary Boycott as Aid to Price Fixing", Yale Law Rev. (Mar., 1922) Vol. XXXI. Pp. 339-342.

"Carlson v. Carpenter's Contractors Association", Illinois Law Rev. (1922) Vol. XVII. P. 534.

"Constitutional Law - Due Process - Equal Protection", California Law Rev.(Mar., 1922) Vol. X. Pp. 237-241.

Gompers, Samuel, "A Legalistic Anaesthetic", American Federationist (Feb., 1922) Vol. XXIX. Pp. 117-119.

Gompers, Samuel, "The Supreme Court at it Again", American Federationist (Jan., 1922) Vol. XXIX. Pp. 44-48.

"Injunctions against Employers Breaking Contracts", Monthly Labor Rev. (Apr., 1922) Vol. XIV. Pp. 818-819.

Kales, Albert M., "Coercive and Competitive Methods in Trade and Labor Disputes", Cornell Law Quart. (Dec., 1922) Vol. VIII. (1) Pp. 1-25, (Feb., 1923) Vol. VIII. (2) Pp. 128-145.

"Picketing & Boycott Cases", American Bar Association Jour. (Feb., 1922) Vol. VIII. Pp. 96-97.

"Primary, Secondary and Tertiary Boycotts", Columbia Law Rev. (June, 1922) Vol. XXIII. Pp. 578-582.

"Secondary Boycotts by Employees of a Common Carrier", Columbia Law Rev. (Dec., 1922) Vol. XX. Pp. 882-886.

"Strikes - Boycotts and Picketing", Minnesota Law Jour.(Mar., 1922) Vol. VI. Pp. 252-253, 333-334.

1923

B. A. A., "Boycott - Action for Damages for Discharges", Illinois Law Rev. (Mar., 1923) Vol. XVIII. Pp. 533-538.

"Boycott of Margarine Products Enjoined", Law and Labor (Nov., 1923) Vol. V. Pp. 313-314.

"Carpenters' District Council Found in Contempt". Law and Labor (Aug., 1923) Vol. V. Pp. 217-219.

"Conspiracy to Exclude a Workman from his Work Enjoined", Law and Labor (Mar., 1923) Vol. V. Pp. 67-68.

1923

J. L. K., "Boycotts - Conclusions or Emotions", <u>Michigan Law Rev.</u>
(May, 1923) Vol. XXI. Pp. 786-788.

1924

"Boycott of Heating and Ventilating Apparatus Enjoined", <u>Law and
Labor</u> (Mar., 1924) Vo. IX. Pp. 52-53.

C. J. T.,"Secondary Boycott. Illinois Law on Right to Immunity",
<u>Illinois Law Quart.</u> (Apr., 1924).

"Destruction of Contracts and Opportunity to Contract Enjoined",
<u>Law and Labor</u> (aug., 1924) Vol. VI. Pp. 223-224.

"Enforcement of 'American Plan' Enjoined", <u>Law and Labor</u> (Mar., 1924)
Vol. VI. Pp. 64-65.

Frey, John P., "An Injunction Case Without a Parallel", <u>American
Federationist</u> (Aug., 1924) Vol. XXXI. Pp. 629-637.

"Interference with Installation of Telegraph Violates Sherman Act",
<u>Law and Labor</u> (Aug., 1924) Vol. VI. Pp. 208-210.

Landis, James M., "Labor's New Day in Court. Jury Trial Vindicated",
<u>Survey</u> (Nov. 15, 1924) Vol. LII. Pp. 175-177.

Pepper, Former Senator, "The Case of Shopmen's Strike", <u>American
Labor Legislation Rev.</u> (Dec., 1924) P. 319.

"Stonecutters' Boycott of Bedford Limestone Held Unlawful", <u>Law
and Labor</u> (May, 1924) Vol. IX. Pp. 109-115.

Union is Citizen of State Where it has Main Office", <u>Law and Labor</u>
(Nov., 1924) Pp. 299-300.

"Verdict against Union for Unlawful Expulsion and Loss of Employment",
<u>Law and Labor</u> (May, 1924) Vol. VI. P. 117.

1925

Chamberlain, Joseph P., "The Legislature and the Labor Injunctions",
<u>American Bar Association</u> (Dec., 1925) Vol. XI. Pp. 815-817.

"Closed Shop Employer Fails to Prove Case", <u>Law and Labor</u> (Aug., 1925)
Vol. VII. Pp. 211-212.

"Forcing of 'American Plan' Reversion of Previous Decision", <u>Law
and Labor</u> (May, 1925) Vol. VII. Pp. 111-115.

"Injunction against Westchester Building Trade Workers", <u>Law and
Labor</u> (Aug., 1925) Vol. VII. Pp. 209-210.

1926

"Boycotting (Sorrel v. Smith, 1925; A.C. 700)", Illinois Law Rev.
(Feb., 1926) Vol. XX. Pp. 591-594; Solicitors' Jour and Weekly
Reports (Feb. 20, 1926) Vol. LXX. P. 394: Harvard Law Rev.
Vol. XXXIX. Pp. 517-518.

"Combination Suppressing Use of Non-Union Made Materials Violates
Law", Law and Labor (Dec., 1926) Vol. VIII. P. 317.

"Mutual Agreement as to Employees Between Employers not Unlawful",
Law and Labor (Nov. and Dec., 1926) Vol. VIII. Pp. 41, 318-319.

1927

"Boycott of Non-Union Made Building Materials Enjoined (Mass.)",
Law and Labor (July, 1927) Vol. IX. Pp. 176-179.

E., G. K., "Refusal of Union Men to Handle Non-Union Made Goods",
Virginia Law Rev.(Dec., 1927) Vol. XIV. Pp. 112-120, 132-133;
Cincinnati Law Rev. (Nov., 1927) Vol. I. Pp. 497-498; Illinois Law
Rev. (Dec., 1927) Vol. XXII. Pp. 444-448.

Green, Wiiliam. "Labor and Injunction", American Federationist
(1927) Vol. XXXIV. P. 1387.

Green, William, "Restraining Lawful Activities", American Federationist (May, 1927) Vol. XXXIV. Pp. 530-531.

Rice, W. G. Jr., "Master - Servant - Sherman Anti-Trust Law",
Wisconsin Law Rev. (July, 1927) Vol. IV. Pp. 250-252, 255.

"Stonecutters' Case on 'Unfair Material'", Yale Law Jour. (Nov,
1927) Vol. XXXVII. Pp. 84-96.

"The Bedford Stone Case - What It Means to American Industry", Law
and Labor (May, 1927) Vol. IX. Law and Labor (Apr., 1927) Vol. IX.
Pp. 77-80.

Witte, Edwin E., "The Journeymen Stonecutters Decision", American
Labor Legislation Rev. (June, 1927) Vol. XVII. Pp. 139-141.

1928

Frey, John P., "The Heart of the Injunction", International Molders
Jour. (April, 1928) Vol. LXIV. Pp. 193-197.

Frey, John P., "Equity - the Great Maverick - Nobody Knows Its
Limits or Powers", International Molders Jour. (May-June, 1928)
Vol. LXIV. Pp. 261-263, 325-326.

"Journeymen Stonecutters Appeal Injunction", Law and Labor (Dec.,
1928) Vol. X. P. 256.

"Law Protects Workers Choosing Own Representatives", Law and Labor
(July, 1928) Vol. X. Pp. 155-156.

1928

Munz, C. Curtis, "The Injunction Proves a Boomerang", <u>Brotherhood of Locomotive Firemen and Enginemen's Jour.</u> (Mar., 1928) Vol. LXXXIV. Pp. 195-197.

"Plasterers Union Enjoined in Secondary Boycott", <u>Law and Labor</u> (Nov., 1928) Vol. X. Pp. 234-236.

1929

"Boycotts - Citizens Committee Enjoined from Coercing Employers", <u>Minnesota Law Rev.</u>(May, 1929) Vol. XIII. Pp. 612-614.

"Boycotts - Legality of Methods Used", <u>Minnesota Law Rev.</u> (May, 1929) Vol. XIII. Pp. 614-615.

"Boycotting an Industry. Louisiana Act Unconstitutional", <u>Monthly Labor Rev.</u> (Jan., 1929) Vol. XXXVIII. Pp. 82-84.

"Campaign of Organized Workers to Destroy Business Held Unlawful", <u>Law and Labor</u> (Dec., 1929) Vol. XI. Pp. 245-250.

"Charge of Blacklisting Good Cause for Action", <u>Law and Labor</u> (Mar., 1929) Vol. XI. P. 56.

"Constitutional Status of Anti-Injunction Laws", <u>Monthly Labor Rev.</u> (Aug., 1929) Vol. II. No. 2. Pp. 106-111.

'Inducing Modification of Contract by Threat of Boycott", <u>Harvard Law Rev.</u> (May, 1929) Vol. XLII. Pp. 960-961.

Kingsley, Robert, "Labor Injunctions in Illinois", <u>Illinois Law Rev.</u> (Feb., 1929) (6): Pp. 529-555.

"Refusal of Preliminary Injunction Sustained", <u>Law and Labor</u> (Jan. & Nov., 1929) Vol. XI. Pp. 11-13 and 226-228.

"Shipowners Central Employment Agency - Not Combination in Restraint of Trade", <u>Law and Labor</u> (May, 1929) Vol. XI. Pp. 99-101.

"Suit for Damages Based on Blacklisting Upheld", <u>Monthly Labor Rev.</u> (June, 1929) Vol. XXVIII. Pp. 1328-1330.

"Union Carpenters Secure Injunction against Citizens Committee", <u>Law and Labor</u> (Feb., 1929) Vol. XI. Pp. 28-30.

1930

"Conspiracy to Restrain Interstate Commerce in Gypsum Products Enjoined", <u>Law and Labor</u> (June, 1930) Vol. XII. Pp. 143-137.

"Court of Appeals Reverses Decision in Case of Aeolin Co. v. Fischer", <u>Law and Labor</u> (May, 1930) Vol. XII. Pp. 102-105.

1930

"Picketing Customers' Place of Business Enjoined", <u>Law and Labor</u>
(June, 1930) Vol. XII. P. 140.

"'Secondary' Strikes, Willson & Adams Co. v. Pierce", <u>Yale Law Jour.</u>
(Apr., 1930) Vol. XXXIX. Pp. 914-915.

1931

"Combination by Electrical Employers and Electrical Union Ousted",
<u>Law and Labor</u> (June, 1931) Vol. XIII. Pp. 123-124.

"Damages for Procuring Discharge Sustained", <u>Law and Labor</u> (May,
1931) Vol. XIII. Pp. 115-117.

"Decrees Enjoining Conspiracy by the Painters' Union", <u>Law and Labor</u>
(Mar., 1931) Vol. XIII. P. 64.

"Injunction not Warranted without Unlawful Acts of Unions", <u>Monthly
Labor Rev.</u> (Sept., 1931) Vol. XXXIII. No. 3. Pp. 77-78.

"Judgment, $43,000, Entered against Labor Unions for Conspiracy",
<u>Law and Labor</u> (May, 1931) Vol. XIII. P. 103.

L., M. I., "Labor Law – Trade Unions – Strikes, Secondary Boycotts",
<u>New York University Law Quart. Rev.</u> (Sept., 1931) Vol. IX. Pp. 99-100.

"Preliminary Injunction Confirmed", <u>Law and Labor</u> (Mar., 1931)
Vol. XIII. Pp. 44-45.

"Secondary Boycott of Machine Made Materials", <u>Columbia Law Rev.</u>
(Jan., 1931) Vol. XXXI. Pp. 156-157.

"Secondary Boycott in Support of Jurisdictional Demand Unlawful",
<u>Law and Labor</u> (Sept., 1931) Vol. XIII. Pp. 210-242.

"Wisconsin Law Relating to Issuance of Injunctions in Labor Disputes",
<u>Monthly Labor Rev.</u> (Aug., 1931) Vol. XXXIII. No. 2. Pp. 53-57.

1932

"Anti-Injunction Laws in Labor Disputes", <u>Monthly Labor Rev.</u>
(July, 1932) Vol. XXXV. No. 1. Pp. 66-88.

"The Strike for the Closed Shop. Massachusetts Precedent", <u>Harvard
Law Rev.</u> (May, 1932) Vol. XLV. Pp. 1226-1230.

"Twelve States Holding Anti-Injunction Labor Laws", <u>Monthly Labor Rev.</u>
(July, 1932) Vol. XXXV.

"Restraint of Trade – Boycotts – Exchanges", <u>Columbia Law Rev.</u>
(Nov., 1932) Vol. XXXII. Pp. 1253-1255.

1933

"Relief Denied Employer Violating Spirit of Labor Laws", <u>Monthly
Labor Rev</u>. (Nov., 1933) Vol. XXXVII. Pp. 1133-1134.

1934

Agger, C., & Eisenberg, E. O., "Equity - Constitutional Law - Labor
Disputes", <u>Marquette Law Rev</u>. (Feb., 1934) Vol. VXIII. Pp. 136-137.

Boudin, L. B., "The Secondary Boycott in New York", <u>St. John's Law
Rev</u>. (Dec., 1934) Vol. IX. Pp. 171-180.

"Courts and the Right to Strike", <u>New Republic</u> (May 16, 1934)
Vol. LXXIX. P. 6.

Crook, W. H., "Revolutionary Logic of the General Strike", <u>American
Political Science Rev</u>.(Aug., 1934) Vol. XXVIII. Pp. 655-663.

G., D. I., "Actionable Interference with Business by Organized Labor",
<u>Temple Law Quart</u>. (Jan., 1934) Vol. VIII. Pp. 245-246.

Henderson, W. B., "Strike Psychology", <u>Common Law Jour</u>. (Nov., 1934)
VOL. XXXIX. Pp. 572-575.

"Injunctions in New Jersey", <u>Nation</u> (Sept. 26, 1934) Vol. CXXXIX.
P. 355.

"Most Oppressive Injunction Granted the Standard Bakery Co., Brooklyn",
<u>New Republic</u> (June 19, 1936) Vol. LXXIX Pp. 111-112.

Paschal, Elizabeth, "The Workers Equity in his Job", <u>American Fede-
rationist</u> (Nov., 1934) Vol. XLI. Pp. 1212-1221; 1332-1342.

Q., P. D., "Labor Law - Strikes, etc. as Affected by N.I.R.A.",
<u>Virginia Law Rev</u>. (Mar., 1934) Vol. XX. Pp. 553-564.

"Social Security and the General Strike", <u>Political Science Quart</u>.
(Sept., 1934) Vol. XLIX. Pp. 411-420.

W., I., "Labor Law - Legality of a Secondary Boycott", <u>New York
University Law Quart</u>. (Mar., 1934) Vol. XI. Pp. 475-476.

1935

Green, B. A., "The Legal Aspects of the Labor Movement", <u>Oregon Law
Rev</u>. (Dec., 1935) (1) Pp. 13-38.

"Labor Law - Secondary Boycott - Picketing Customers of Non-Union
Manufacturer", <u>Columbia Law Rev</u>. (Mar., 1935) Vol. XXXI. Pp. 456-457.

"Labor's Charter of Rights", <u>American Federationist</u> (Apr., 1935)
Vol. XLII. Pp. 361-408.

1935

Laidler, H. W., "America in the Depression and Under the New Deal",
Social Action (May 15, 1935) Pp. 1-31.

McGabe, J. A., "Strikes - Boycotts - Right to Join a Union", Notre
Dame Law (Jan., 1935) Vol. X. Pp. 205-209.

Mongold, W. C., "On the Labor Front", New Republic (Mar. 13, 1935)
Vol. LXXXXII. P. 131.

1936

"Competitive Torts - Trade Boycotts - Boycott of Non-Member",
Columbia Law Rev. (Mar., 1936) Vol. XXXVI. Pp. 484-487.

****

PART II

B. NEWSPAPERS

Newspapers have always been a useful source of information in writing a history of, or preparing a bibliography on any subject. It would have been desirable to include all newspapers dealing with the boycott but for many reasons this has been impossible.

The New York Times has been selected as the best medium for the purpose of this bibliography because it supplies a fairly continuous study of the labor struggles of the United States. It is especially valuable, as with the exception of the years 1905-1912 inclusive, it has a fully recorded index. Much that has been written on earlier struggles is taken from second and third hand reports, here we have information written on the spot as well as contemporary opinion.

THE NEW YORK TIMES INDEX

1885

Jan. 25   Central Union Advise boycotting. 8:3

Mar. 25   Orange: Boycotting F. Berg & Co. 3:1, 29- 9:3

Aug. 19   Gould Railroad System. Especially Wabash. Knights of Labor's orders. 1:5, 21- 2:6, 22- 4:7, 23- 1:4, 24- 5:5, 25- 1:4, 27- 2:5

    28   Knights of Labor boycott Wabash Rolling Stock. 8:2

    30   Boycotting discontinued. 7:5, 31- 1:5

Sept. 4   Knights of Labor's Conference with Manager Talmadge. 5:1, 5- 2:4, 8- 1:7

Nov. 5   Mallory Steamship Company's Employees' Boycott. 4:7, 6- 5:5, 7- 1:7, 8- 1:5, 9- 5:4, 10- 1:5, 11- 1:4, 12- 2:3, 13- 1:7

    15   "Boycott" as used by employers and employees. Stratton & Storm's Case. Ed. **8**:5, 17- 4:2, Dec. 8- 4:5, 26- 4:4

1886

Jan. 16   Chicago Shoe Manufacturers employing prison labor boycotted by Knights of Labor. 1:2

    29   Galveston, Texas. Mallory Steamship Co. Boycotted by Knights of Labor. 1:4, 30- 1:4, 31- 6:7, Feb. 2- 1:4

Feb. 9   "Boycotting" generally discussed. Ed. 4:3

    11   Chicago laborers boycott firms selling prison made goods. 3:4

Feb. 18   F. B. Thurber, Boycotted by Cigarmakers. 2:7

Mar. 27   Stonecutters (headed by G. Crawford) on refusal to join
           Bluestone Dealers Assoc. 8:5

     28   Lynn Boycott. 9:3

Apr. 9   Mrs. E. A. Gray's Bakery on Hudson St. boycotted. 8:5, 10-
           3:2, 11- 2;4 and 3:5, 13- 8:1, 14- 8:1, 15- 8:1, 16- 8:1, 17-
           5:5, 18- 3:1, 20- 8:2, 21- 8:1, 24- 8:1. Picketers arrested.
           Justice Duffy censured by Central Labor Union, Apr. 19- 5:3

     16   Cavanagh, Sanford & Co. Tailors:- 35 boycotters arrested.
           8:5, 25- 9:3, 27- 5:1, 28- 8:2

     16   New Haven. Advertisers of Courier & Journal Boycotted by Typo-
           graphical Union No. 47. Injunction argued. 1:6, 18- 3:6

     18   Boycott of Landgraf's Bakery. 2:6, 20- 8:2, 21- 8:1, 22- 5:4,
           23- 2:5, 24- 8:1, 25- 9:3, 28- 8:2, 29- 2:2, 30- 1:4, May
           1- 8:4, 4- 4:7, 6- 5;5, 7- 8:5, 9- 9:1, 13- 8:2, 15- 3:1, 22- 3:2.
           June 4- 2:7, 5- 8:5, 29- 2:5, 20- 5:6.
           Indictments and arrests, May 6- 5:5, May 7- 8:5

     18   Times Financial Article on Boycotting. 9:4

     24   Theiss's Alhambra Saloon boycotted by Carl Sahm Club. 21 arrests.
           Trial: 8:1,, 30- 8:3, May 1- 2:5, 2- 1:5, 5- 2:2, 6- 5:2, 7- 8:5.
           Trial: Convictions Apr. 24- 8:1, June 23- 3:1, 24-1:7, 29 and 30
           8:1

     29   B. F. Glidden arrested: Trial, 1:7, May 1- 1:2

May 1   Boycotters: Justice Welde censured by Grand Jury for refusal
           to indict. 8:1

     3   Boycotters and Rioters under indictment. Central Labor Union
           engages Gen. R. A. Pryor to defend. 8:3

     4   Boycott: Lozanos, Pendas & Co. 4:7

     13   Glidden and others fined. 1:2, June 17- 1:4

July 17   Boycott on Ehret's Beer. Sequel of Theiss' Saloon Case.
           Sympathy with Crime. Ed: 4:2, 20- 4:5, 22- 4:5. Central Union de-
           clared unjust. Dec. 14- 6:2. Ed.

     18   Boycotting: New Haven Journal, Conviction. 6; 1

     20   Boycotters of Theiss's Saloon: Sentences Commuted. Ed:
           4:2, Oct. 12- 4:1

     23   Richmond, Va. Baughman Bros. Boycotted by Labor Herald.
           T. R. Wiles' Petition for injunction granted. 5:2

1886

July 29   Agitation by strikes and boycotts. Injury to the poor shown. Ed: 4:4

Aug.   6   Salem, Mass. W. B. O'Keefe & P. McGeogh. Trial on F. Emery's charges. 3:2

      15   Cleveland Leader Boycotted by Typographical Union. 1:6

      21   M. J. Storen, boycotted by Bricklayer's Union No. 7. 8:6

Sept. 10   Boycotters convicted in New York City District Attorney Martini's Views, 8:5, 11- 8:4

      18   New York City: Bohemian Baker's Union: Persecution of P. Max for aiding boycotted Mrs. Landgraf. 8:2

1887

July 15   Universal Amusement League's Boycott of F. & F. Morse. 8:6

Aug.   1   District Assembly No. 30 asks Central Union's aid in boycotting Batcheller's Shoe Factory in North Brookfield, Mass. 2:2

      12   Hanan & Son, Shoe Manufacturer's threaten lock-out as a boycott reprisal, 8:3, Sept. 30- 8:3, Nov. 18- 4:7

      28   F. Meyer and C. Pfeifer boycotted by Bakers Union No. 1, Quartlinger & Bode arrested, 9:1

      31   S. Brenner boycotted by Mason's Union. Arrested for conspiracy. 8:4

Oct.   9   Convictions for conspiracy by Washington Court. Fines. 4:7

Nov. 17   Musician's Case in Washington, J. A. Callen to be tried by jury. 5:1

      19   Terrace Garden: Boycotted for employing non-union men. 8:1

Dec.   8   Boycott of West Springfield Post Office, Ed. 4:1

      15   American Federation of Labor Convention: Brewers of Milwaukee, St. Louis & N. Y. boycotted: 15- 9:2, 16- 2:5, 17- 5:3, 18- 9:2

1888

Jan.   4   Boycott of Milwaukee Beer by Brewers' Workers' Union. Ed. 4:5

      4   Boycott of Milwaukee Beer by Brewers' Workers' Union. 9:4

Feb.   9   Boycotting Milwaukee Beer by United States Brewers Association. 3:2

1888

Mar.   6   Conspiracy Law settled in Case of Hanan and Gardiner & Estes' Foreman Hartt, 8:5

      12   Engineers (Division No. 49) boycott freight arriving at East St. Louis. 1:3

      17   Boycott Division: Pittsburgh. Brace Brothers, damage suit. 3:7

      24   Freight Boycott raised. Engineers attempt to make deal with Knights of Labor. 1:4, Apr. 5- 5:1

      28   Brewers refusal to recognize Journeymen's Union. (Ed.) 4:2

Apr.   4   Boycott of Q. Freight. Enforcement of Inter-State Commerce Law punishing it urged. (Ed.) 4:3, 5- 4:3, 8- 4:1

      13   N. Y. City Brewers' Lockout against Knights of Labor Journeymen. (Ed.) 4:17, 17 and 18- 4:5, 19 and 21- 4:4

      27   Arbitration Boards Investigation. (Ed.) May 2- 4:6

June 4   Boycott of Pool Beer by Central Labor Union. 8:4, 25- 8:1

       5   Pool Beer consumed by Central Labor Union Members while under boycott. Union Beer neglected. (Ed.) 4:4, 6- 4:4

      23   Hartt sues Assembly No. 91 for damages for compelling discharge by Gardiner and Estes. 9:4

July 13   Walking delegates tried for conspiracy to prevent O. M. Hartt's employment and to procure discharge. (Ed.) 4:5, 18- 4:5

      13   Conspiracies and boycotts. Law interpreted in case of O. M. Hartt, gardiner and Estes Foreman. 5:6

Aug. 4   J. L. Hudson boycotted for permitting non-union band to bear name. 1:2

      29   Conspiracy Law: Rochester Tumbler Company's suit against Secretary Dillon of American Flint Glass Workers' Association. 2:6

Sept. 28   New York Law against Conspiracy - Workingmen's attempt to have it repealed. (Ed.) 4:3

Nov. 28   Boycott of Stevenson's Brewery by union men. Master Ale Brewers' Association Action. 8:3, 29- 8:3

      29   Brewers defeat boycotters. 4:5

1889

Jan. 4   Central Union of New York. Bribery to raise Pool Beer boycott charged. 2:1, 7- 8:2

<u>1889</u>

Feb. 18 Boycott on Pool Beer. Appointment of special committee to investigate bribery charges, causes Socialists to resign. 5:1, 25- 4:7

Mar. 8 Brewers' strike in New York City. S. Weiss shot by J. Probanski for enforcing boycott. 2:4

June 25 Rockwell's Bakery boycotted by strikers in Bakers' Union. 8:4

<u>1890</u>

Aug. 8 Brick Manufacturers of Verplanck's boycotted to force employment of union men. (Ed.) 4:4, 19- 4:5, 25- 4:4, 26- 4:3, 28- 4:1, 30- 4:3, Sept. 9- 4:4, 16- 4:5, 28- 4:1, Oct. 5- 4:2

    24 "Rights When Organized": Discussion apropos of New York Central Strike and Brick Boycott. (Ed.) 4:2

Sept. 29 Boycott of Peck, Martin & Co.'s Building Materials by trade unions in N. Y. C. 13:7. Oct 1- 8:5, 2- 8:6, 3- 9:3, 4- 9:3

Nov. 24 Boycott raised from Pool Beer. 5:4

Dec. 5 Boycott of Edelsteins: Bakers: 8:5

     6 Judge Wilde's Action denounced by Central Labor Federation. 8:5, 8- 5:7

<u>1891</u>

Mar. 28 Knights of Labor - Order to Boycott. Rochester Clothing Manufacturers. 1:2

Apr. 28 Felsenkeller boycotted by Carl Sahm Club for employing A. Weichert. His share in Theiss convictions. Appeal to District Attorney. 5:3, 29- 9:3, May 11- 2:4, 12- 9:1

May 12 Bucki's Lumber boycotted: Lumber Dealer's Association's lockout against Lumber Handlers' Union: Board of Walking Delegates. 9:4, 14- 10:2 and 1:4, 19- 2:5, 21- 6:2, 22- 6:3 23- 3:2, 24- 3:7, 27- 8:5, June 5- 8:2

    14 Bucki's Lumber boycotted. Buffalo and Tonawanda Lumber Association tenders aid. 1:4

    14 Boycott of Pelzer's Beer Garden, for employing E. Schert by Carl Sahm Club, also other cases. (Ed.) 4:4

    22 New York City Lumber boycott. Likeness to brick boycott. Walking Delegates tyranny. (Ed.) 4:4, 23- 4:6, 24- 4:1

1891

Aug.   13   Anheuser-Busch Company of St. Louis: Boycott. 1:2,
               Oct. 1- 8:5

       24   Tinplate Rollers imported for Mr. Niedringhaus' Factory.
               Boycott for Wage Agreement Violation.   (Ed.) 24, 25, 27,
               28 and Aug. 1- 4:2, Aug. 3- 4:3, 21- 4:3, 22- 4:1, Oct. 11-
               4:5, 26- 4:4

Dec.   19   Ehrets' Beer boycotted by the American Federation of Labor.
               3:4

1892

Jan.   27   St. Louis: Anheuser-Busch & Lemp Breweries boycotted by
               workmen. 1:4, May 17- 8:3

Feb.   27   Bill before New York Legislature to legalize boycotts. 8:4

Aug.   6   South Bend: Studebaker's Works boycott Carnegie Steel Mills.
               5:3

Sept. 19   Central Union, Boycott of Brewer George Ehret agitated. 8:7

1893

Mar.   21   Conspiracy and Boycott Law. Toledo, Ann Arbor and North
               Michigan and Lake Shore Railroad Cases. Refusal to receive
               freight. Injunction suit decision. (Ed.) 4:3, Apr. 5- 4:2

       21   Toledo, Ann Arbor and North Michigan Engineers: Brotherhood
               Chief Arthur enjoined from interfering with traffic. Decision
               by Judge Taft. (Ed.) 4:3, 30- 4;2, Apr. 4 and 5- 4:2

       26   United Garment Workers - Cutters' Union No. 4 lockout. 2:4
               28- 8:5

Apr.   2   Boycotting circulars enjoined. 11:2, 5- 6:5

       3   Unions: Strikes and boycotts drive away better element and
               popular sympathy. (Ed.) 4:3

       4   Lake Shore Engineers' refusal to handle freight. Judge Rick's
               Decision. Appeal. Comments by Messrs Ashley and Gompers. 8:1

       4   Boycott by Brotherhood of Locomotive Engineers. Injunction suit.
               Judge Taft's opinion. Appeal. Comments by Messrs. Ashley and
               Gompers. 8:1

       6   Manufacturers Association's Petition for injunction refused by
               Judge Barrett. 8:5

       7   Injunction Decision: Text of Order of the Court. 5:3

       7   Lake Shore requested to reinstate Brotherhood Engineers. 5:3

<u>1893</u>

Apr.   8   Cutters'Damage Suit. 8:5

      14   Cutters Conference with Manufacturers. 2:3

      15   Brotherhood of Locomotive Engineers' Suit to compel Georgia
              Central R.R. to make contract. Judge Speer's adverse decision
              influenced by Anti-Trust Law. Comparison with Judge Riner's
              Decision. (Ed.) 4:4

      18   N.Y.C. Clothing Cutters' Union-Manufacturers' Lockout. Boy-
              cotting should be punished. Litigation. 4:1. Ends without
              securing objective. (Ed.) Apr. 25- 4:2

      21   Boycott-Union. Railroad Elevator Company suit against Carrington
              & Co. for injuring trade. 11:2

      21   End of boycott. 1:3, 23- 3:4

<u>1894</u>

Mar. 24   Boycott of Brooklyn Brewery. P. McMenamy and others arrested
              for distributing circulars. 9:2

Apr. 27   Brewers refuse to sign contract with Brewery Employees' Union
              No. 69. 9:4

May   7   Brewers lockout against Knights of Labor. 1:4

      12   Pullman: Car Works Men. 8:3, 13- 5:5

      16   Pullman: Petition to Congress. 3:2

June 23   Chicago: Pullman Cars boycotted by American Railway Union.
              1:2, 24- 17:3, 26-8:4, 27- 8:1, 28- 1:3, 29- 1:5, 30- 1:3

July 1   American Railway Union: Universal boycott resulting from
              Pullman strike. (Ed.) July 1, 2, 3, 4, 7- 4:2

       5   Federal Government's and Court's Duty in Pullman boycott.
              (Ed.) 4:2

       5   Mr. Pullman refuses to arbitrate. California Militia Mutiny.
              (Ed.) 4:1

       6   Debs Statement. (Ed.) 4:1

       9   Central Union and Federation (N.Y.C.) and District 49 in-
              dorse Debs boycott. Apropos of Pullman strike. 1:1

Sept. 15   Boycott of Brooklyn Brewery for refusal to employ Knights of
              Labor. (Ed.) 4:2

<u>1894</u>

Sept. 15   Boycott of Budweiser Brewing Company by United Brewers Assoc. 9:3, 23- 12:2

Dec. 16   Wallace Building: Carpenter J. E. McDonald boycotted by walking delegates. 5 indictments. 6:4

17   Carpenters' United Brotherhood Delegates indicted for preventing men from securing work. (Ed.) 4:5

<u>1895</u>

Jan. 8   Eugene V. Debs - Indictment for conspiracy. Judge Grosscup refuses to Quash. 15:5

8   Chicago: Pullman Palace Cars boycotted, Debs and American Railway Union sentenced for contempt. 15:5, 9- 8:4

17   Pullman boycotted. Writ of error petition refused. Jan. 22- 16:2, bailed.

25   Debs: Trial for conspiracy. 15:2, 26- 10:7, 29- 14:5, 30- 10:4, Feb. 1- 15:2, 5- 8:5, 7- 5:4, 8- 1:2, 12- 5:2, 13- 14:5

Feb. 8   G. M. Pullman's contempt of subpoena. 1:2, 13- 14:5, 14- 1:6

Apr. 29   Trial discussed. 1:5

Aug. 29   American Railway Unions' (1894) Boycott of Pullman Co.'s Cars. Judge Tafts' address before American Bar Association. 4:1

<u>1896</u>

May 22   Milwaukee Street-Railway Employes. Cars boycotted. 1:1, 25- 5:3, 26- 4:6, June 5- 5:6, 20- 1:6

Aug. 4   Braunworth, Munn & Barber & E. Ives & Son: Books boycotted by International Brotherhood of Book Binders. 8:1

<u>1897</u>

Nov. 14   Boycott: Use Illegal. Kansas Court's Decision in Oxley Stone Company's Case. 9:1

15   Oxley Stone Company boycotted by Cooper's Union. Kansas Court's Decision against legality. (Ed.) 4:2

<u>1898</u>

Feb. 7   Central Union of Brooklyn. Reporter's boycotted. 5:5

1899

Mar. 19   Labor conspiracy Laws: Non-union engineer dismissed upon United Portable Hoisting Engineers' demand. Judge Kellog's decision contrary to Penal Code. (Ed.) 18:2

Aug. 1   Cleveland Street-Railway boycott effective. Mobs beat prominent citizen. 3:6, 2- 3:3, 3- 3:4, 5- 1:3

     10   Anti-boycott meeting. 2:2

1900

Apr. 16   Cigarmakers discharge 10,000 employees. 2:5

     30   Labor defies injunction and delegates denounce Justice Freedman (Cigarmakers). 8:4

May   6   Alliance meeting in Cooper Union. 11:4

      9   Justice Freedman's decision denounced. 7:7

June 6   Justice Fitzgerald dissolves Justice Freedman's injunction. 14:3

1901

July 6   Tailors' United Brotherhood, N.Y.C. 2:6

     21   Tailor's fight middleman. 1:5

     22   Tailor's fight spreading. 2:4, 23- 3:4, 24- 2:6

     25   Tailor's ultimatum. 14:6

     26   Mass meeting-Hamilton Fish Park. 8:1

     27   Small manufacturer's threatened. 14:5

     28   Agreements signed. 9:3

     30   Lockout. 12:1

     31   Dead-Lock. 12:2

Aug. 8   Pickets arrested. 2:2

      9   Tailors Stone Shops in Brooklyn. 2:2

Nov. 10   Chicago: Tailors boycott enjoined, 5:5

1902

Apr. 2   Right to boycott affirmed. Judge Parker's Text. 4:2

1902

Apr. 4   Right to conspiracy: Court of Appeals on Steamfitters.
           (Ed.) 8:3

      8   Boycott unlawful. Wilkes-Barre. 1:5

May 20   Boycott legal in Missouri. 2:4

June 5   Boycotts Scabs. Miners boycott of non-union men and fami-
           lies in Wilkes-Barre. 1:3

     30   Right of conspiracy. Wisconsin decision. (Ed.) 8:3

Nov. 15   Trolley boycotted. 1:2

     17   Boycott facts. 1:7, 18- 1:7

1903

July 3   Texas sues Herff boycotters. 1:2

Sept. 10   Chicago: Boycott suit of Stiles. 7:1

      13   Danbury boycotters sued. 11:3

Oct. 14   Boycott injunction by Judge Belden, Hamilton, Ohio. 5:2

Nov. 11   Anti-boycott Society's Work. 2:5

     13   Anti-boycott Association-Danbury Case. 6:3

Dec. 20   Chicago funerals boycotted. 1:3

     24   Chicago teamsters. 8:3

1904

Aug. 14   Boycott derided- Beef Trust and Market Wagon Driver's Union.
           Typhoid danger. 16:5

     22   Kosher boycott. Sympathy with strikers. 2:5

Dec. 17   Boycott legal-Appellate Division on Stereotypers v. Brooklyn
           United States Printing Co.

....

"LAPSE of TIMES INDEX FROM 1905 - 1912, INCLUSIVE"

....

1913

Nov. 5   American Federation declared to be a labor trust by Tom
           Mann. Samuel Gompers denounces statement. 8:8

1920

Nov. 10   Injunction suit brought by Burgess Bros. co. to make permanent
            injunction restraining various labor unions from refusing to
            handle lumber shipment at S.S. piers and R.R. terminals because
            of Co.'s rejection of demands of Lumber Handlers Union. 21:2

1921

Jan. 4   Secondary Boycott- U. S. Supreme Court decides unions are not
            immune from prosecution and judicial restraint in their inter-
            ference with interstate commerce of employers. Grants injunc-
            tion to Duplex Co. 1:1

      5   S. Gompers assails decision. 10:5

      5   (Ed.) Labor, Society and the Law. 12:3

      6   F. Morrison criticises decision. 25:3

      7   V. S. Gauthier hints at united action by organized labor against
            Supreme Court decision. 2:6

Feb. 27   M. Woll says A.F. of L. will have bill introduced providing
            against all anti-combination and so-called Conspiracy Laws. 19:1

Mar. 1   Executive Council drafts bill to escape Anti-Trust Law. 3:4

      2   Mathew Woll sees gain to labor in U. S. Supreme Court decision
            on Lever Act - says it may end conspiracy cases. 15:6

May   6   American Federation of Labor - Open Shop- Samuel Gompers says
            unions can meet issue, at Cincinnati meeting of Executive
            Council. 14:5

      11   Secondary Boycott - Cohen, Freedlander & Martin Co., obtain
            temporary injunction to restrain International Ladies Garment
            Workers' Union from conducting strikes against their business
            associates. 4:2

June 14   American Federation of Labor - Open Shop - Samuel Gompers says
            it has failed, at Denver convention. 1:3

      18   Union Labels - Delegates reject proposal to search members and
            eject those wearing unlabeled clothing. 7:2

Aug. 25   American Federation of Labor - Samuel Gompers, researchers. on
            charges of industrial conspiracy. 12:3

1922

Feb. 26   American Federation of Labor - Open Shop - Executive Council of
            Federation of Labor orders inquiry into suspected activities of
            banks - Washington Conference. 14:8

June 7   Boycott of Labor Unions - F. Morrison complains to Attorney
            General Daugherty that certain dealers in building materials in
            San Francisco have refused to sell to firms employing union
            labor. 4:3

Apr. 28 Pennsylvania Railroad - Labor - Labor Board will issue decision indicting Pennsylvania Railroad for failure to comply with Board's ruling issued July 19, 1921, ordering Railway to hold new election of employees to represent shop crafts. 28:3

29 Pennsylvania Railroad & Labor. Labor Board cites new violation of its ruling. Part II, 6:3

May 21 President Rea notifies Labor Board Pennsylvania Railroad will not be represented at hearing on complaint of Brotherhood of Railway and Steamship Clerks. 24:1

22 Labor Board summons Rea as a witness in case brought by Clerks' Union. 28:2

29 Rea says Pennsylvania Railroad will adhere to refusal to allow Clerks' Brotherhood to name representatives for election at Labor Board hearing. 6:2

June 18 Labor Board formally rebukes Railway for its defiance of unions, condemns employee representation plan. 1:4

25 Labor Board's rebuke ignored by shopmen, who use Railways' employee representation plan in election of representatives. 25:3

28 Labor Board rebukes Pennsylvania Railraod for persistent violation of court's decision in contempt of law and of United States Court rulings and opinion of Congress, its decision on election of Clerks' representation. 6:1

29 President Rea says Pennsylvania Railroad obeys valid laws created by properly constituted authority, in reply to Labor Board's denunciation. 19:8

29 B. M. Manly. Director of Peoples Legislative Service, urges President Harding to declare Federal boycott against Pennsylvania Railroad because of disregard of Board's Ruling. 19:8

July 2 The Railraod and the Board. 14:4

Oct. 14 Labor and Pennsylvania Railroad employees conference with President Coolidge. Explain company union plan. Sec. I, Part II. 5:6

20 Clerk's Brotherhood files suit in equity to prevent adjustment of grievances by company union. Hearing set for November 2nd. 17:8

25 Labor Board rules company must conform to Board's decision. 32:1

Nov. 1 E. Lee explains industrial adjustment plan, at N. Y. C. convention of American Management Association. 35:1

3 Shop craft employee sue for $15,000,000, alleged underpayment of wages resulting from Pennsylvania Railroad's refusal to abide by Labor Board's rules. 15:5

1923

Nov. 10   Jurisdiction of Labor Board to order reinstatement of car inspector denied by Pennsylvania Railroad ignoring decision. 22:2

      25   Brotherhood of Railway Clerks states legal points in case against Railway, charges Company obstructs purposes of Transportation Act. Sec. II. 1:1

Dec. 15   Pennsylvania Railroad rebuked by Labor Board for alleged violation of its decisions. 14:4

      22   Judge Dickinson dismisses suit brought be Brotherhood of Clerks, Frieght Handlers and Station Employees to compel Pennsylvania Railroad to obey order of the Labor Board and recognize delegates of Brotherhood as representative of employees in conference on wages and working conditions. 20:5

      23   Clerks' Brotherhood files notice of appeal to U.S. Circuit Court from decision dismissing suit to compel recognition. 2:3

      23   H. T. Hunt, Attorney for Clerks' Brotherhood, explains their application for injunction against Railway Company Union. Sec. II. 12:3

1924

Mar.   1   United States Attorney Buckner files petition to restrain 5 unions, Westchester County Building Trades, and 16 Union officials from preventing use in New York City and environs of cast stone made at a lower cost outside the City by union and non-union men. A. P. Royce estimates increased costs due to restrictions. 1:4

      23   Closed Shop - Massachusetts Superior Court rules Milk Drivers and Creamery Workers Union must pay damages for illegal strike to enforce employment of Union Labor - Famous Danbury Hatters Case recalled. 1:2

Apr. 22   Theater owners alarmed by rapid growth of Theater Treasurers Union, A.F. of L. Managers warn box office employees that membership will mean dismissal. 10:1

      25   Sherman Anti-Trust Law assailed by Samuel Gompers at convention of National Civic Federation. 16:8

June   4   U. S. Circuit Court dismisses indictment on charges of conspiracy in restraint of trade found against M. S. Colleran and officers and members of the Plasterers' Union based on testimony taken at Lockwood Company inquiry. 11:2

July   8   Justice Lydon denies request of S. Untermeyer for 10 days delay to prepare defense of International Association of Bridge, Structural & Ornamental Iron Workers, against which Iron League seeks an injunction to end strike. 14:1

       9   International Association files counter suit for $10,000,000 damages charging conspiracy to destroy union. Mr. Lane, counsel for employees. Untermeyer defends strikes. 10:1

1924

July 13   Brooklyn Court issues injunction restraining United Building Common Laborers' Union from interfering with International Bricklayers' Helpers' Union. 3:6

15   Federal Judge Thomas refuses to dismiss injunction brought by J. I. Hass, Inc. against Brotherhood of Painters, Decorators, and Paperhangers of America in dispute on wage scale for work on Conde Naste Company's plant at Greenwich, Conn. 8:7

15   Pennsylvania Road wins labor suit. Conspiracy not proven. 8:8

16   Justice Benedict denies plea of International Bricklayers' Helpers' Union for temporary injunction to restrain United Building and Common Laborers Union of America from interfering with International members. 4:3

25   Iron League loses fight for injunction. 14:1

Aug. 11   American Federation of Labor plans campaign to promote purchase of goods bearing Union Labels. 15:8

24   Boycott of non-union products, planned by Central Union Label Council of N. Y. C. 30:4

1925

Feb. 8   Union Men watch, as precedent, Court's decision in suit brought by Philadelphia Electrotypers' and Finishers Union and International Stenotypers and Electrotypers Union against Bethlehem Plate Co. and J. M. Davis for alleged violation of contract to work only in union shops. (Indirect boycott?) Sec. IX, 6:2

23   C. L. Eidlitz predicts bad results from edict of Electrical Workers Union in Cleveland and St. Louis, that members will install only lighting fixtures wired by union labor. 32:1

22   Judge Young enjoins Building Trades Council of Westchester County and its affiliated labor unions from carrying on an alleged conspiracy against Willson Adams Co. of Mt. Vernon and 28 other building material firms in Westchester County. 31:4

1926

Aug. 21   P. J. Carpenter Jr. obtains temporary injunction restraining Westchester County Building Trades Council official from interfering with his business. 3:3

1927

Mar. 29   Federal Judge Thacher rules that association of stone workers which have been trying to keep cast stone made outside metropolitan area from entering the district, have been guilty of restraining trade in violation of Sherman Law and of conspiracy. Enjoins them from further interference with construction of building. Decision in case begun in 1925 by Decorative Stone Co. of New Haven, Conn. 11:2

1927

Apr. 12   Anti-Trust Law. U.S. Supreme Court sustains injunctions against
             Stonecutters Unions for acting in restraint of trade. Unions
             held subject to Anti-Trust Law. 12:1

1929

Oct. 16   Injunction on Labor Disputes. National Association of Manu-
             facturers convention warned by J. A. Emery on impending legis-
             lation. 13:4

      18   A. Furuseth amd M. Woll clash on program for legislature. 14:2

      19   A. Furuseth casts only dissenting vote in endorsement of injunc-
             tion bill. 2:4

      19   Judge Thacher denies piano manufacturer a writ against Organ
             Workers Union. (Ed.) 18:1

      21   F. H. LaGuardia claims introduction of first Anti-Injunction
             Bill in Congress. 2:4

      27   Feature article on Anti-Injunction Bill designed by American
             Federation of Labor to assure workers right to strike, picket
             and combine. Sec. X, 5:1

Nov. 21   Injunction in labor disputes defended by W. G. Merritt in
             speech at convention of National Founders Association. 36:1

      26   Injunctions used against striking produce truck drivers in
             Newark by 38 merchants. 24:4

Dec.   5   Anti-Injunction Act proposed by New York State Federation of
             Labor. 10:2

      25   Judge E. O. Lewis invalidates injunction issued 10 years ago
             in Building Trades, Philadelphia. 38:8

1931

Jan. 12   J. W. Gerard advocates legislation to control use of injunction.
             Assails use of "Yellow Dog" contract as basis. 31:1

Aug. 15   Executive Council of American Federation of Labor draws up a bill
             for presentation to Congress: would legalize boycotts, benefit
             payments and peaceful propaganda. 2:4

Oct. 11   Pennsylvania Supreme Court upholds "Yellow Dog" contract
             forbidding unionization under penalty of discharge. 24:4

      16   Labor use of boycotts. 22:6

1932

Jan. 28   Norris Anti-Injunction Bill. 2:6, 30- 36:3, Feb. 5- 39:3, 16-
10:7, 24- 37:1, 26- 5:1, 27- 29:8, Mar. 2- 20:3, 3- 2:5, 9- 10:7,
10- 2:5, 17- 37:7, 18- 9:1, 19- 16:2, 24- 37:4, 26- 12:3.

May 29   C. L. Greeves says even name of "Yellow Dog" contract, is an
attempt at intimidation. Defends right to make individual
contracts. 11:6

1935

National Biscuit Co. Boycott:

Jan. 9   3000 strike in sympathy withPhiladelphia group. 3:6

11   Conference fails to reach a settlement. (Parties-Regional
Board, Representatives of the Company and Inside Bakers Federal Union.) 27:8

12   Grocery stores picketed. 2:3

16   2 hurt in strike in Newark. 19:2

20   Parade in New York City. 27:4

22   Six arrested. 2:4

23   Three jailed. 13:2

26   13 strikers fired, Linden, N. J. 14:7

27   Union appeals to Washington. 17:7

28   Bureau of Labor Statistics completed survey to help in dispute over Codes. 22:6

Feb. 6   National Biscuit Co. strikers attack truck. 5:3

12   Disorder marks re-opening. 3:4

22   21 arrested as pickets and workers clash. 3:3

23   3 arrested for assault on non-union worker. 3:3

24   Strikers charge assault by company guards. 23:6

26   Two strikers hurt. 9:2

Mar. 7   Strikers picket home of O. L. Mills. 17:3

14   National Biscuit Co. stockholders meet to discuss strike. 39:3

17   Brooklyn Church and Mission Federation reveals National Biscuit
Co. asked aid of pastors. Sec. II, 1:3

28   Company seeks injunction against picketing by Inside Bakery
Workers Federal Union and $100,000 damages. T. I. Sheridan
presents Union's grievances. 38:3

II-50

<u>1935</u>

<u>National Biscuit Co. Boycott:</u>

Mar. 29   N. I. R. B. approves amendments to code for semi-handicraft shops and maximum work week of 44 hours. 42:1

Apr. 4   Strikers reject proposal of 45% of strikers to return to work and several hundred strike-breakers to remain. 2:6

7   Court enjoins strikers from activities-former Senator Sheridan defends them. 37:2

11   Ten strikers seized in clash with police. 9:1

12   Correction. 18:3

12   3 arrested as strikers - try to storm police lines protecting workers. Commissioner Valentine orders inquiry into charges of "unnecessary force." 18:2

14   Knitgoods Workers Union protest to LaGuardia. 26:1

18   Mr. G. Pinchot leads picket parade. 18:5

19   7 arrested during picket demonstration against workers. 2:2

29   Strike ends in N.Y.C. and Philadelphia. 3:2

30   Unions sign agreement. 11:5

May 2   38:3, 8- 5:5, 13- 4:2, 14- 12:6, 20- 6:2.

****

Aug. 29   N.Y. Supreme Court upholds the rights of persons charged with contempt of court for violating labor injunctions to demand trial by jury. Case of Standard Baking Co.v. Local 505, Bakery & Confectionary Workers International Union of America. 14:2

Dec. 1   Labor on Economic boycott enforced 135 years ago by T. Paine's "Association of Nations", Sec. IV, 9:1

PART THREE

DOCUMENTS

Caldwell, Henry Clay
     Dissenting opinion of Mr. Chief Justice Seth Shepart of the Court of
     Appeals of the District of Columbia, in the contempt case of Gompers
     v. Buck's Stove and Range Co. Trial by Judge and Jury. Washington.
     American Federation of Labor. 1909.

Christenson, Jacob et al v. Kellogg Switchboard & Supply Company.
     Brief, Argument and Decision of Appellate Court of Illinois. Chicago.
     Anti-Boycott Association, 1903.

Circuit Court of the United States, District of Columbia.
     Dietrich E. Loewe and Martin Fuchs v. Martin Lawlor et al. Brief for
     Plaintiff on demurer to complaint. Bridgeport, Conn., Buckingham,
     Brewer & Platt Co. 1906.

Court of Appeals of the District of Columbia.
     American Federation of Labor et al, appellants v. Buck's Stove and
     Range Co., appellee. Brief for appellee. October Term. Washington.
     1908.

Court of Appeals of the District of Columbia.
     Buck's Stove and Range Co. v. The American Federation of Labor, et al.
     Arguments in contempt proceedings by Alton B. Parker, J. H. Ralston,
     J. J. Darlington and J. M. Beck. New York. American Anti-Boycott
     Association. 1909.

Massachusetts. Committeee on Relation between Employer and Employee.
     Blacklisting, intimidation, boycotts, injunctions on labor disputes.
     Pp. 56-73, Appendices 11, 12, 13, 15. Boston, Wright & Porter
     Printing Co. 1904.

Massachusetts Attorney General's Office.
     Opinion of Attorney General, relative to the constitutionality of
     a Bill to make lawful certain agreements between employees and laborers
     and to limit the issuing of injunctions in certain cases. Massachusetts.
     General Court Legislation. December, 1914.

William Howard.
     Decisions rendered by the Honorable William Howard Taft, in cases
     coming before him as judge, in which were involved questions affecting
     boycotts, labor injunctions, organizations and the Federal Anti-Trust
     Law (Superior Courts). Washington. Ludworth & Co. 1908.

United States Anti-Injunction Bill.
     Complete hearings before the Committee on the Judiciary of the House of
     Representatives on H. R. 89. 54th Congress, 1st Session, 1904.
     Washington. Government Printing Office, 1904.

United States Bureau of Labor.
     Sixteenth Annual Report 1901. Pp. 871-1036. "Decisions of courts and
     laws relating to strikes, combinations, conspiracies, boycotts, etc.".
     Washington. Government Printing Office, 1901.

United States Bureau of Labor.
    Twenty-first annual report 1906. Pp. 917-960. "Strikes, boycotts and
    blacklisting, etc." Washington. Government Printing Office, 1906.

United States Bureau of Labor.
    Twenty-Second Annual Report of Commissioner of Labor. 60th Congress,
    1st Session, 1907. House Document No. 982. Washington. Government
    Printing Office, 1907.

United States Bureau of Labor.
    Bulletin No. 18. Buck's Stove and Range Co. v. The American Federation
    of Labor. Pp. 10124-10138. Washington. Government Printing Office, 1909.

United States Bureau of Labor.
    Bulletin 22. Pp. 667-670. Meier v. Speer. Washington. Government
    Printing Office, 1911.

United States Bureau of Labor Statistics.
    Bulletin No. 112, 152, 169, 189, 224, 246, 258, 290, 309, 344, 391,
    417, 517. Washington. Government Printing Office, 1912.

United States Circuit Courts.
    Decision of Judge Speer of Georgia, Judge Ricks of Ohio and Judge Taft
    of Ohio, in certain cases involving rights and duties of railroad em-
    ployees, and construction of the Anti-Trust and Interstate Laws. 53rd
    Congress, Special Session. Senate Miscellaneous Document 47. Washington.
    Government Printing Office, 1893.

United States Courts.
    Federal Anti-Trust decisions. Cases decided in the United States Courts
    arising under, involving or growing out of the enforcement of the Anti-
    Trust Act of 1890 (26 Stat. 209) including a few similar decisions not
    based upon it, (1890-1899). See Combinations, Conspiracies and Labor
    Organizations. Compiled under direction of Attorney General J. A. Finch.
    Washington. Government Printing Office, 1907.

United States House of Representatives. Committee on the Judiciary, 54th
Congress, 2nd Session.
    House Report No. 2471. Contempts of Court. Report of the Committee on
    the Judiciary, January 8th, 1907. Washington. Government Printing
    Office. 1897.

United States House of Representatives. Committee on the Judiciary, 54th
Congress, 2nd Session.
    House Report No. 2471, Part 2. Views of the minority. January 11th, 1897.
    Washington. Government Printing Office, 1897. Reprinted in (Senate
    Document No. 190. 57th Congress, 1st Session, Pp. 5-10.)

United States House of Representatives. Committeee on the Judiciary, 54th
Congress, 1st Session.
    House Report No. 1987. Submitted by Mr. C. E. Littlefield. The meaning
    of the word "Conspiracy", etc. June 5, 1900. Washington. Government
    Printing Office, 1900.

United States House of Representatives. Committee on the Judiciary. 54th
Congress, 2nd Session.
>   Senate Document No. 58. Reprinted in the Senate Document No. 190.
>   57th Congress, 2nd Session, Pp., 11-85. Report on a hearing before
>   the Committee, March 25, 1900, on the bill "to limit the meaning of the
>   word 'Conspiracy' and also the use of 'restraining' order and 'injunc-
>   tion' as applies to disputes between employers and employees in the
>   District of Columbia and territories and engaged in commerce between
>   the several states, District of Columbia and territories and with
>   foreign nations." December 20, 1900 - Ordered to be printed to accom-
>   pany S4233. Washington, Government Printing Office, 1900.

United States House of Representatives. Committee on the Judiciary. 56th
Congress, 1st Session.
>   House report No. 2007. "The meaning of the word 'Conspiracy' etc."
>   Report to accompany H. R. 8917. Washington. Government Printing
>   Office, 1900.

United States House of Representatives. Committee on the Judiciary. 56th
Congress, 1st Session.
>   House report No. 2007, Part 2. Limit the meaning of the word "Con-
>   spiracy". Feb. 4, 1901. Washington. Government Printing Office,
>   1901.

United States House of Representatives. Committee on the Judiciary. 57th
Congress, 1st Session.
>   House report No. 1522. Limiting the meaning of the word "conspiracy"
>   Report to accompany H.R. 11060, 1902. Washington. Government Printing
>   Office, 1902.

United States House of Representatives. Committee on the Judiciary. 57th
Congress, 1st Session.
>   House report No. 1522, Part 2. Views of the minority. Government
>   Printing Office, 1902.

United States House of Representatives. Committee on the Judiciary. 57th
Congress, 1st Session.
>   House report No. 1522 (See pp. 354-391.) Anti-Injunction Bill. Complete
>   hearing before the Committee on the Judiciary of the House of Representa-
>   tives on the Bill(H.R. 89) entitled "a bill to limit the meaning of the
>   word 'conspiracy' and the use of 'restraining' orders and 'injunction'
>   in certain cases." Jan. 13-Mar. 22, 1904. Washington. Government
>   Printing Office, 1904.

United States House of Representatives. Committee on the Judiciary. 60th
Congress, 1st Session, 1908.
>   Argument with Mr. Gompers, regarding use of injunction in labor dis-
>   putes. Printed by order of the Committee. Washington. Government
>   Printing Office, 1908.

United States House of Representatives. Committee on the Judiciary. 60th
Congress, 1st Session, 1908.
>   Argument of Mr. T. C. Spelling in favor of the so-called "anti-injunc-
>   tion" bills and all labor bills. Washington. Government Printing
>   Office, 1908.

United States House of Representatives. Committee on the Judiciary. 60th
Congress, 1st Session, April 4 - May 1, 1908.
     An Act to regulate commerce, etc. Hearings on House Bill 19745, before
     subcommittee No. 3, of the Committee on the Judiciary of the House of
     Representatives. Hepburn amendment to Sherman Anti-Trust Act of 1890,
     Charles E. Littlefield, Chairman of the sub-committee. Washington.
     Government Printing Office, 1908.

United States House of Representatives. Committee on the Judiciary.
     Hearings on the so-called Anti-Injunction Bill and all labor bills.
     Arguments of Spelling, Gompers, etc. - John J. Jenkins, Chairman.
     Printed by order of the committee. Washington. Government Print-
     ing Office, 1908.

United States Industrial Commission.
     Report on legislation (Commissioner's Reports, Vol. V.) General
     and convict labor, mine labor, enforcement of contracts, strikes,
     boycotts, pickets, etc. Washington. Government Printing Office,
     1900.

United States Industrial Commission.
     Final report prepared in accordance with an Act of Congress approved
     June 18, 1898. The Commission's Report, Vol. XIX. Washington.
     Government Printing Office, 1902.

 United States Industrial Commission.
     Reports on Labor Organizations, labor disputes and arbitration (by Clarke
     E. Edgarton and E. Dana Durand.) Railway Labor, by Samuel McCune Lindsay.
     Laws and Court Decisions as to labor combinations. Pp. 114-125, 567-627.)
     Table of citations, general considerations; English law on strikes and
     labor combinations, legality of strikes, enticement of employees, com-
     binations to procure, cischarge or prevent employment, intimidation,
     picketing, boycotts. Railway strikes and boycotts, (a) General principles
     laid down by courts. (b) Specific acts and methods of strikers held ille-
     gal by the courts. (c) Legislation as to strikes on railways.
     Injunction in labor disputes (a) Court decisions as to injunctions
     (b) legal cirticisms on the extended use of injunctions. Legal position
     of Trade Unions. Commissions Reports Vol. XVII. Washington. Government
     Printing Office, 1901.

United States Industrial Commission.
     Report of the Industrial Commissioner. Vol. XIX, Part 1, Chapter 3.
     See also Vol. V, VIII, XII, XIV, XV, XVII. Washington. Government
     Printing Office, 1902.

United States Industrial Commission.
     Industrial report, Vol. XI. P. 10654. Report of Commissioner
     Lennox. Washington. Government Printing Office, 1916.

United States Senate, Committee on the Judiciary. 54th Congress, 1st
Session.
     Senate Report No. 827. Report to accompany S-2984 on the subject of
     "Contempt of Courts", as enforced by the Federal Courts, Apr. 30,
     1896. (Reprinted in Senate Document No. 190, 57th Congress, 1st Session,
     Pp. 3-4.) Washington. Government Printing Office, 1896.

United States Senate 1901-1902. 57th Congress, 1st Session, Senate
Document No. 190.
    Compilation of documents relating to injunctions in conspiracy
    cases also arguments and decisions of the court in case of Common-
    wealth v. Hunt. Feb. 13, 1902. Washington. Government Printing
    Office, 1902.

United States Senate. 57th Congress, 1st Session, Senate Document No.
278.
    Anti-Injunction Bill. Letters from various labor organizations
    relating to the substitution of Senate Bill No. 4553 for the Hoare
    Anti-Injunction Bill S-1118, April 1, 1902. Washington. Govern-
    ment Printing Office, 1902.

United States Senate. 57th Congress, 2nd Session, Senate Document No.
115.
    Petition and remonstrances for and against the passage of the bills
    (S-1118; S-4553 and H.R. 11060), "To limit the meaning ot the word
    'conspiracy' and the use of 'restraining' orders and 'injunctions'
    in certain cases, with a list of organizations so petitioning."
    Washington. Government Printing Office, 1903.

United States Senate. 60th Congress, 1st Session.
    Congressional Record Vol. XLII, Part 5, Pp. 4846-4859. "Regulation of
    Injunctions: Debate on Senate Bill 3732, regulating injunctions and
    practice of District and Circuit Courts of United States," April 17,
    1908. Washington. Government Printing Office, 1908.

United States Senate. 60th Congress, 1st Session. 1907-1908.
    Certain injunctions and labor cases. Papers (60th Congress 1st
    Session, Senate Document No. 504.) Washington. Government Printing
    Office, 1908.

United States Senate. Committee on the Judiciary.
    Federal Injunctions. Hearing before a sub-committee of the Committee
    on the Judiciary, United States Senate, on the Bill S-3724, a bill re-
    gulating Injunctions and the practice of the District and Circuit
    Courts of the United States (Jan. 27 - Feb. 3, 1910.) Washington.
    Government Printing Office, 1910.

United States Senate. Committee on the Judiciary. 62nd Congress, 3rd
Session, 1913.
    Hearings before a sub-committee of the Committee on the Judiciary
    of the United States Senate, 62nd Congress, 3rd Session, on H. R.
    23635, 1913. Washington. Government Printing Office, 1913.

United States Senate. Committee on the Judiciary. 67th Congress, 2nd
Session, May 2, 1922.
    Amending section 266 of judicial code, report to accompany S-3040
    (relating to injunctions based on the unconstitutionality of State
    laws,) submitted by Overman. Senate report 682, 67th Congress, 2nd
    Session, Vol. II, P. 7951.

United States Strike Commission. 1894.
    Report on the Chicago Strike of June - July, 1894, with appendices
    containing testimony, proceedings and recommendations. Also pu-
    blished as: (Senate Executive Document No. 7, 53rd Congress, 3rd
    Session.) Washington. Government Printing Office, 1895.

Supreme Court of the District of Columbia.
  <u>Buck's Stove and Range Co., plaintiffs v. American Federation of
  Labor et al, defendants, in equity, No. 27305. Copies of affidavits
  filed by plaintiff for use on hearing or application for a temporary
  injunction.</u> St. Louis, 1907.

Supreme Court of the District of Columbia.
  <u>Buck's Stove and Range Co., Plaintiffs v. The American Federation
  of Labor et al. Filed December 18, 1908. Opinion of Justice Wright.</u>
  Washington. Government Printing Office, 1908.

Supreme Court of the District of Columbia.
  <u>Buck's Stove and Range Co., Plaintiffs v. The American Federation of
  Labor et al, Defendants. Petition to have Samuel Gompers adjudged
  guilty of contempt.</u> St. Louis, 1908.

Supreme Court of the District of Columbia.
  <u>Buck's Stove and Range Co., Plaintiffs v. The American Federation of
  Labor et al, Defendants. Arguments in support of petition to have
  Samuel Gompers adjudged guilty of contempt.</u> New York. "American
  Anti-Boycott Association, 1909.

Supreme Court of the District of Columbia.
  <u>Buck's Stove and Range Co., Plaintiffs v. The American Federation of
  Labor et al, No. 27305, in equity. Decision of Justice Wright in contempt proceedings against Samuel Gompers, adjudging them guilty of
  contempt of court - together with newspaper editorials, expression of
  the country thereon.</u> New York. American Anti-Boycott Association,
  1909.

Supreme Court of the District of Columbia.
  <u>Petition of Buck's Stove and Range Co. for an order against Samuel
  Gompers, Frank Morrison and John Mitchell, to show they should not
  be punished for the Court's injunction of Dec. 18, 1907.</u> Washington.
  American Federationist, Sept., 1908. Vol. XV. Pp. 674, 678, 680,
  682, 684, 686, 690, 692.

Supreme Court of the District of Columbia.
  <u>Dietrich E. Loewe and Martin Fuchs, Plaintiffs in error, v. Martin
  Lawlor et al, Defendants in error. Brief for plaintiffs in error.</u>
  October Term, 1907. New York. C. G. Burgoyne, 1907.

Supreme Court of the District of Columbia.
  <u>Decision of Justice Gould of the Supreme Court of the District of
  Columbia, granting a preliminary injunction in the Buck's Stove and
  Range Co. v. The American Federation of Labor.</u> New York. American
  Anti-Boycott Association, 1910.

Supreme Court of New York.
  <u>Joseph Michaels, Morley A. Stern et al., Plaintiffs, v. Sidney Hillman,
  individually and as president of the Amalgamated Clothing Workers of
  America, et al., Defendants. Memorandum of Law.</u> New York. Hecla
  Press, 1920.

Supreme Court of the United States.
    Buck's Stove and Range Co., appelant, v. American Federation of
Labor, appellees. October Term, 1910. No. 190. American Federation
of Labor et al, appellants v. Buck's Stove and Range Co., appellees,
No. 394. Briefs for Buck's Stove and Range Co. Washington. B. S.
Adams, 1910.

Supreme Court of the United States.
    October Term, 1910. No. 190. The Buck's Stove and Range Co., ap-
pellants v. The American Federation of Labor, appellees. No. 394.
The American Federation of Labor et al, appellants v. Buck's Stove
and Range Co., appellees. Brief on behalf of the American Federation
of Labor et al. appellees in No. 190 and appellants in No. 394.
Washington. Judd and Deitweiler, Inc., 1910.

Supreme Court of the United States.
    October Term, 1910. No. 190. The Buck's Stove and Range Co. v.
The American Federation of Labor et al, appellee. No. 372 (or old
No. 685); Samuel Gompers, John Mitchell and Frank Morrison, peti-
tioners v. The Buck's Stove and Range Co., respondents. Brief in
reply to appellant's brief in No. 372 Or (old 685). New York.
William Ficks Co., 1910.

PART FOUR

STATUTES

The indexes of very few of the compiled statutes or codes of the various states carry any reference of boycott. The term boycott ordinarily means a confederation, sometimes secret, of persons whose intent is to injure another by preventing any and all persons from doing business with him. Neither at common law nor under statutes modifying the common-law doctrine is it lawful to combine to injure another's business by causing his employees to leave his service by intimidation, threats, or coercion, and such a combination constitutes an indictable conspiracy. Hence the action of boycott is founded generally in conspiracy to perform an illegal act or to perform a legal act through illegal means, and therefore the references here, in the main, are to the sections of conspiracy in the statutes. At common law the conspiracy was complete when the agreement to do the illegal act was reached. As modified by the statutes, an overt act is generally required. The overt act which might evidence a boycott is sometimes itself prohibited by a seperate statute, such as one forbidding interference with employment, intimidation, and picketing.

Alabama Code of 1928	Chapter 91. Sec. 3447 et seq. (Conspiracy to prevent carrying on business, picketing to induce others not to trade, etc.)
Arizona Struckmeyer Rev. Code 1928	No specific provision. (Sec. 4286 denies right of injunction in controversies between employers and employees, unless necessary to prevent irreparable injury to property.)
Arkansas Crawford & Moses, Digest of Stats. 1921	No specific provision.
California General Laws 1931	Penal Code, Ch. VIII, Sec. 182, Conspiracy Act 1605 - limits the meaning of the word "conspiracy" and also the use of "restaining" orders and "injunctions", in disputes between employers and employees.
Colorado Courtright's Mills annotated statutes. 1925	Chapter 18 - Secs. 464, 465, 466, Blacklisting and boycotting. (Unlawful to induce others not to trade; print or circulate notice of boycott, etc.)
Connecticut Rev. Stat. 1930	Offenses against public peace and safety. Ch. 327. Sec. 6208. (Intimidation; boycotting.)
Delaware Rev. Code 1915	No specific provision.
Dist. of Columbia Code. 1929	No specific provisions.

Florida Compiled General Laws 1927	Fifth Div. Ch. VI. Act 8, Sec. 7541, Conspiracy (Sec. 7542 Combinations to prevent persons from working, causing dis- charge etc. prohibited.)
Georgia Park's Annotated Code 1914	Fourth Division. Article 15, Secs. 126, 127, 128, 129. (Conspiring, attempting to interfere with business or labor by threats, intimidation.)
Idaho Code Annotated 1932	Penal Code - Title 17 - Ch. 10; -17-1027. Conspiracy (Ch. 215, session Laws 1933, declaring public policy of Idaho regarding labor organizations specifically, among other things exempts boycotts in strikes from restraining orders and injunctions.)
Illinois Revised Stats. 1935	Criminal Code. Ch. 38. Sec. 116. Conspiracy (Establishing boycott or blacklist; posting or distri- buting written notice of it, etc.)
Indiana Burns Ind. Stats. Anno- tated 1933	Criminal offenses. Ch. 11, Sec. 10-1101. Conspiracy (Conspire to wrongfully injure, etc.)
Iowa Code 1935	Ch. 586, 13162 - Conspiracy (Conspire to wrongfully injure, etc.)
Kansas Rev. Stats. 1923	Ch. 44. Art. 6, Secs. 44-617. Labor & Industries (Conspiring or inducing to quit employment, picketing, etc.)
Kentucky Carroll's Stats. 1930	No specific provision.
Louisiana Dart's Gen'l Stats. (Supp. 1935)	No specific provision. (But note Sec. 4379.5 et seq. title XXXIV. Labor & Industry Ch. 9A. Contracts in restraint of labor membership contrary to public policy, etc. jurisdiction of courts to issue in- junctions in labor disputes, limited.)
Maine	Ch. 138, Secs. 126, 127. (Conspiracy wrongfully to injure business or property and by force or intimidation interfering with employment.)
Maryland Bagby's Anno. Code -1924 Supp. 1935	Crimes and Punishments. Art. 27. Sec. 43A-43 (Conspiracy.) (Agreements, in furtherance of trade disputes, excepted as not conspiracy.)
Massachusetts General Laws 1932	Labor and Industries. Ch. 149. Sec. 19 and 24. (Interferring with employment; actionable conspiracy.)

Michigan   No specific provision.
Compiled   (But Ch. 154, Sec. 8612 provides penalty for interfering
Laws   with employees.)
1929

Minnesota   Ch. 96, Sec. 10055. Conspiracy (Interfering or threatening
Mason's Stats.   to interfere with trade, business, property, etc.)
1927   (Sec. 10056 states, cooperation to obtain increased wages,
                  peaceably, is not conspiracy.)

Mississippi   Ch. 20, Sec. 830. Conspiracy
Code   (Interfering with trade, property, etc. by force, intimi-
1930   dation.)

Missouri   Ch. 30. Sec. 4243. Conspiracy; Sec. 4246. Interference
Stats.   with employment by threats, etc.
1931

Montana   Ch. 14, Sec. 10898. Conspiracy.
Rev. Codes
1921

Nebraska   Crimes and Punishment. Ch. 28-813.
Compiled Stats.   (Inducing or influencing not to trade.)
1929

Nevada   Sec. 10061. Conspiracy (Sec. 10062 makes over tact
Hillyer's Stat.   unnecessary.)
Laws. 1929

New Hampshire   No specific provisions.
Public Laws
1926

New Jersey   Conspiracy - Sec. 37, p. 1757.
Compiled Stats.
Supp. to 1930

New Mexico   No specific provisions.
Statutes 1929

New York   Penal Law. Article 54. Conspiracy Sec. 580, Par. 4
McKinney's Con-   (Maintenance of boycott against business.)
solidated Law
1928. Supp. 1935

No. Carolina   Conspiracy, p. 174.
Jerome's Crim.
Code & Digest
1934

No. Dakota   Penal Code. Ch. 17. Conspiracy Sec. 9441.
Compiled Laws   (Interference with use of property or trade by force.)
1925

Ohio
Patterson's
Crim. Law
1929

No specific provision

Oklahoma
Stats. 1931

Crimes and Punishments. Ch. 15, Art 32 - Sec. 1960 - 5th
  (Act injurious to trade or commerce - but Ch. 52 - Art. 4-
Sec. 10878 - specially exempts acts in furtherance of trade
disputes between employers and employees.)

Oregon
Code 1930

Title XIV - Ch. VIII - Section 14-860
  (Crimes against public policy, trade and economy.)

Pennsylvania
Purden's
Stats. 1936

Crimes and Offenses - Title 18 - Sec. 2451.
  (Conspiracy to do unlawful act.)

Rhode Island
General Laws
1923

Chapter 396 - Sec. 9 (6054)
  (Of offenses against the Public Peace and Property.)

So. Carolina

Article 14 - Sec. 6636
  (Conspiracy to defraud by boycotts, etc., limiting competition in trade.)

So. Dakota
Comp. Laws
1929

Crimes. Sec. 3598. Conspiracy.
  See also Sec. 4373 -4374 (Intimidating laborers and
employees.)

Tennessee
Code 1932

Section 11064 - (7) Conspiracy
  (Act injurious to trade or commerce.)

Texas
Stats. 1928

No specific provision.
  (See Ch. 10 of Penal Code Sec. 1094 et seq. interfering with
workers, intimidating etc. - those engaged in leading, un-
loading and transporting commerce in the State.
This so-called "Open Port Law" - 1925 was held unconstitutional
in Ratcliff v. State 289 S.W. 1072 violative of 14th Amendment
of the Constitution of the United States as class legislation
for failure to make specific intent to hinder commerce the
essential element, as act provides penalty for ordinary
assault on employee of common carrier in excess of penalty for
assault on other classes of persons.

Utah
Rev. Stats.
1933

Penal Code. Ch. 11 - Conspiracy 103-11-1 (5)
  (See Title 49 - Labor - 49-2-3. Unlawful to induce labor to
quit work or to refuse to work by means of force.)

Vermont
Public Laws
1933

Crimes and Offenses. Title 37 - Ch. 344 - Sec. 8590-1
  (Intimidation of workmen, to stop work.)

Virginia
Code
1930

No specific provisions.

Washington
Remington's
Rev. Stats.
1933

Criminal law. Title 14 – Ch. 5 – Sec. 2382. Conspiracy
 (Labor Law – Title 50 – Ch. 2 – Sec. 7611 et seq. legalizes
labor unions, restricts injunctive relief in labor disputes
unless necessary to prevent irreparable injury, and prohibits
prosecutions for entering into agreements and combinations to
lessen hours, increase pay or better working conditions.)

West Virginia
Code 1931

No specific provisions.

Wisconsin
Stats.
1933

Offenses against property – Ch. 343 – 681
 (restraint of will to compel another act.)

Wyoming
Rev. Stats.
1931

No specific provisions.
 (Ch. 63 – Article 2 – No injunction permitted in labor
disputes, where fraud or violence is not shown. No court
shall issue restaining order or injunction on ground that
persons participating in labor dispute constitutes an unlawful
combination or conspiracy.)

CASES

PART V

SECTION I

ALPHABETICALLY ARRANGED

-A-

Aikens v. Wisconsin, 195 U. S. 914, 25 Sup. Ct. 3, 49 L. ed. 154. (1904).

Allis Chalmers Co. v. Iron Molders' Union, 150 Fed. 155. (1906).

American Steel & Wire Co. v. Wire Drawers' and Die Makers' Union, 90 Fed.
     598. (1898).

Arthur v. Oakes, 63 Fed. 310, 11 C.C.A. 209, 25 L.T.A. 414. (1894).

Axton Fisher Tobacco Co, v. Evening Post Co., 169 Ky. 64, 183 W.S. 269.
     (1916).

Bailey v. Master Plumbers', 103 Tenn. 99, 52 S.W. 853. (1899).

Baldwin v. Escanaba Liquor Dealers' Assn., 165 Mich. 98, 130 N.W. 214.
     (1911).

Banks v. Eastern R. and Lumber Co., 46 Wash. 610, 90 Pac. 1048. (1907).

Beechley v. Mulville, 102 Iowa 602, 70 N.W. 107, 63 Am. St. Sp. 479.

Belfi v. United States, 259 Fed. 822, 170 C.C.A. 622. (1919).

Bement v. National Harrow Co., 186 U.S.,70. (1902).

Bitterman v. L. & N. R.R., 207 U.S., 205. (1907).

Block v. Standard Distilling etc.,Co., (c.c.) 95 Fed. 978. (1899).

Board of Trade v. Christie, 198 U.S., 236. (1905).

Bohn Mfg. Co. v. Hollis, 54 Minn. 223, 55 N. W. 1119. (1893).

Booker & Kinnaird v. Louisville Bd. of Fire Underwriters, 188 Ky. 771,
     224 S.W. 451. (1920).

Boyle v. United States, 40 Fed. (2d) 49. (1930).

Bowen v. Matheson, (14 Allen) 499, 96 Mass. (1867).

Brewster v. C. Miller's Sons Co., 101 Ky. 368, 41 S.W. 301. (1897).

Carew v. Rutherford, 106 Mass. 1, 8 Am. Rep. 237. (1870).

Carter v. Fortney, 170 Fed. 463. (1908).

Chiatovich v. Hanchett, 88 Fed. 873. (1898).

Chicago W. and V. Coal Co. v. People, 214 Ill., 421. (1905).

Chipley v. Ackinson, 23 Fla. 206, 1 So. 934. (1887).

Citizen's etc. Co. v. Montgomery Light and Water Power Co., 171 Fed. 553.
          (1909).

Clark v. Sloan, 37 P. (2nd) 263 (Okla) (1934).

Cleland v. Anderson, 66 Neb. 252, 92 N.W. 306, 96 N. W. 212, 98 N.W. 1075.
          (1912).

Coeur D'Alene Consol. Min. Co. v. Miners' Union, 51 Fed. 260, 19 L.B.A.

Collins v. American News Co., 34 Misc. (N. Y.) 260, 69 N.Y. Supp. 638. (1901).
          aff. 68 App. Div. 639, 74 N.Y. Supp. 1123. (1902).

Commonwealth v. Hunt, 4 Metc. (45 Mass.) 111, (1842).

Continental Insurance Co. v. Fire Underwriters, 67 Fed. 310. (1895).

Cornellier v. Haverhill Shoe Manufacturers Assn., 211 Mass. 554. (1915).

Cudahy Packing Co. v. Frey & Son, 261 Fed. 65, 171 C.C.A. 661. (1919).
          aff. 260 U.S. 568, 43 Sup. Ct. 210, 67 L. Od. 408.
          (1923).

Dagostino v. Rogers, 68 Pa. Sup. Ct. 284. (1917).

Dade Enterprises v. Vometco Theaters, 160 Fla. So. 209. (1935).

Denver Jobbers' Assn. v. People, 21 Col. App. 326, 122 Pac. 404. (1912).

Deon v. Kirby Lumber Co., 162 La. 671. (1927).

Dick v. Northern P. R. Co., 86 Wash. 211, 150 Pac. 8. (1915).

Downes v. Bennett, 63 Kan. 653, 66 Pac. 623. (1911).

Dueter Watch Case Mfg. Co. v. E. Howard Watch and Clock Co., 66 Fed. 637,
          14 C.C.A. 14. (1895).

Dunlap's Cable News Co. v. Stone, 15 N.Y. Supp. 2. (1891).

Eastern States Retail Lumber Dealers' Assn. v. United States, 234 U.S. 600,
          34 Sup. Ct. 951, 58 L. ed. 1490. (1914).

Ellis v. Innman, Poulsen & Co., 131 Fed. 182, 65 C.C.A. 488. (1904).

Emack v. Kane, 34 Fed. 46. (1888).

Ertz v. Produce Exchange, 79 Minn. 140, 81 N.W. 737. (1900).

Federal Trade Commission v. Gratz, 253 U.S. 421, 40 Sup. Ct. 572, 64 L. ed. 993. (1920).

Federal Trade Commission v. Raymond Bro. Clark Co., 263 N.S. 565, 44 Sup. Ct. 162, 68 L. ed. 448. (1924).

Finnegan v. Butler, 112 Misc. 280, 182 N.Y. Supp. 671. (1920).

Funck v. Farmers' Elevator Co., 142 Iowa 621, 121 N.W. 53. (1909).

Gatzon v. Bruening, 106 Wis. 1, 81 N.W. 1003. (1900).

Gibson v. Fidelity & Casualty Co., 232 Ill. 49, 83 N.E. 539. (1908).

Gladish v. Kansas City Live Stock Exchange, 113 Mo. App. 726, 89 S.W. 77. (1905).

Graham v. St. Charles St. R. Co., 47 La. Ann. 214, 16 So. 806. (1895).

Great A. and P. Tea Co. v. Cream of Wheat Co., 224 Fed. 566; aff. 227 Fed. 46, 141 C.C.A. 594. (1915).

Green v. Samuelson, 178 Md. A. 109. (1935).

Greer v. Stoller, (c.c.) 77 Fed. 1. (1896).

Grenade Lumber Co. v. Miss, 217 U.S. 433, 30 Sup. Ct. 535, 54 L. ed. 826. (1910).

Griffin v. Palentine Ins. Co., 238 Texas S.W. 637. (1922).

Guethler v. Altman, 60 N.E. 355. (1901).

Gulf etc. R. Co. v. Miami Steamship Co., 86 Fed. 407. (1898).

Hackney v. Fordson Coal Co., 230 Ky. 362. (1929).

Hailey v. Brooks, 191 S.W. 781. (1916).

Hart v. B. F. Keith Vaudeville Exchange, 12 F. (2nd) 341. (1926).

Hartnett v. Plumbers' Supply Assoc., 169 Mass. 229, 47 N. E. 1002. (1897).

Hawarden v. Youghiogheny & L. Coal Co., 111 Wis. 545, 87 N. W. 472. (1901).

Heim, Fred Brewing Co. v. Belinder, 97 Mo. App. 64. (1902).

Heywood v. Tillson, 76 Me. 225, 46 Am. Rep. 373. (1883).

Hindley v. Louisville R. R., 105 Ky. 162. (1899).

Hunt v. Simonds, 19 Mo. 583. (1854).

In re Debs, 158 U.S. 564. (1895).

In re Lennon, 166 U.S. 548. (1897).

Jackson v. Stanfield, 137 Ind. 592, 36 N.E. 345. (1893).

Jayne v. Loder, 149 Fed. 21, 78 C.C.A. 653. (1906).

Kellogg v. Sowerby, 190 N.Y. 370, 83 N.E. 47. (1907).

Kinloch Tel. Co. v. Local Union No. 2, 265 Fed. 312. (1920).

Klingel's Pharmacy v. Sharp & Dohme, 104 Md. 218, 64 Atl. 1029. (1906).

Knapp-Monarch Co. v. Anderson, 7 F. Supp. 332. (1934).

Knauer v. United States, 237 Fed. 8. (1916).

Labor Review Pub. Co. v. Galliher, 153 Ala. 364, 45 So. 188. (1907).

Lamar v. United States, 260 Fed. 561. (1919).

Langley v. Furman, 230 N.Y. S. 538, 132 Misc. Rep. 726. (1928).

Lawrence Trust Co. v. Sun-American Pub. Co., 245 Mass. 262, 139 N.E. 655.
            (1923).

Leech v. Farmers Tobacco Warehouse Co., 171 Ky. 791, 188 S.W. 886. (1916).

Lewis v. Hine-Hodge Lumber Co., 121 La. 658, 46 So. 685. (1908).

Lewis v. State, 4 Ala. App. 141, 58 So. 802. (1912).

Locker v. American Tobacco Co., 106 N.Y. Supp. 115, 121 App. Div. 443.
            (1907). aff. 115 N.Y. 5 5, N.E. 2. (1909).

London Guarantee Co. v. Horn, 206 Ill. 493. (1904).

Lucomsky v. Palmer, 252 N.Y. S. 529, 141 Misc. Rep. 278. (1931).

Ludwig v. Western Union Tel. Co., 216 U.S. 146. (1910).

Macauley Bros. v. Tierney, 19 R.I. 255, 33 Atl. 1. (1895).

Martineau v. Foley, 225 Mass. 107, 113 N.E. 1038. (1916); 231 Mass. 220,
            120 N.E. 445. (1918).

Master Builders Assn. v. Domascio, 16 Colo. App. 25, 63 Pac. 782. (1922).

McBride v. United States, 234 U.S. 600, 34 Sup. Ct. 951, 58 L. ed. 1490.
                    (1914).

McCarter v. Chamber of Commerce, 126 Md. 131. (1915).

McDonald v. Ill. C.R.R., 187 Ill. 529, 58 N.E. 463. (1900).

McGee v. Collins, 156 La. 291, 100 So. 430. (1924).

McMaster v. Ford Motor Co., 122 S.O. 244, 115 S.E. 244. (1921).

Mennen Co. v. Federal Trade Comm., 288 Fed. 774, 30 A.L.R. 1120. (1923).

Metcalf v. American School-Furniture Co., 108 Fed. 909. (1901).

Miller v. Post Pub. Co., 266 Pa. 533, 110 Atl. 265. (1920).

Mines v. Scribner, 147 Fed. 927. (1906).

Montague v. Lowry, 193 U.S. 38, 44 Sup. Ct. 307, 48 L.ed. 608. (1904):
                    aff. 115 Fed. 27, 63 L.R.A. 58, 52 C.C.A. 621. (1902).

Montgomery Ward & Co. v. South Dakota Retail Merchants' & Hardware Dealers'
                    Asso., 150 Fed. 413. (1907).

Munter v. Eastman Kodak Co., 28 Cal. App. 660, 153 Pac. 737. (1915).

National Fireproofing Co. v. Mason Builders' Assn., 169 Fed. 259, 94 C.C.A.
                    535. (1909).

New York Ice Co. v. Parker, 21 How. Pr. 302. (1861).

Olive v. Van Patten, 7 Tex. Civ. App. 630, 25 S.W. 428.

Orr v. Home Mutl. Ins. Co., 12 La. Ann. 255, 68 Am. Dec. 770. (1857).

Pacific Typesetting Co. v. International Typographical Union, 125 Wash.
                    273, 216 Pac. 358. (1923).

Palatine Ins. Co. v. Griffin, Tex. 202 S.W. 1014. (1918).

Park, John D. & Sons Co. v. National Wholesale Druggists Assn., 50 N.Y.
                    Supp. 1064. (1896).

Payne v. Western & A. R. Co., 13 Lea. 507, 49 Am. Rep. 666. (1884).

Peek v. Nothern P. R. Co., 51 Mont. 295, 152 Pac. 421. (1915).

People v. Sheldon, 139 N.Y. 251. (1893).

Pidcock v. Harrington, 64 Fed. 821 (1894).

Post v. Southern R.R. Co., 103 Tenn. 184. (1899).

Pratt Food Co. v. Bird, 148 Mich. 631. (1907).

Purington v. Hinchcliff, 219 Ill. 159, 76 N.E. 47. (1906).

Raycroft v. Tayntor, 68 Vt. 219. (1896).

Raycroft v. Plumbers' Material Protective Assn., 30 Misc. 709, 63 N. Y. Supp.
                303. (1900).

Rice v. Albee, 164 Mass. 88, 43 N.E. 122. (1895).

Robertson v. Parks, 76 Md. 118. (1892).

Robinson v. Texas Pine Land Assn., 40 S.W. 843. (1897).

Rockwood Corporation of St. Louis v. Bricklayers' Union No. 1 of St.
                Louis, 35 F. (2d) 25, (Cortiorari denied, 50 S. Ct. 30).
                (1929).

Rohlf v. Kasemeier, 140 Iowa 182, 118 N.W. 276. (1908).

Roseneau v. Empire Circuit Co., 131 App. Div. 429. (1909).

Rourke v. Elk Drug Co., N. Y. 75 App. Div. 145, 617. (1902).

Rowan v. Butler, 171 Ind. 28, 85 N.E. 714. (1908).

Schulten v. Bavarian Brewing Co., 96 Ky. 224, 28 S.W. 504. (1894).

Scully v. Bird, 209 U.S. 481. (1908).

Singer Sewing Machine Co. v. Lang, 186 Wis. 530, 203 N.W. 399. (1925).

Smid v. Bernard, 31 Misc. (N.Y.) 35, 63 N.Y. Supp.278. (1900).

Southern Indiana Exp. Co. v. United States Exp. Co., (c.c.) 88 Fed. 659.
                (1898).

Standard Oil Co. v. Doyle, 118 Ky. 662, 82 S.W. 271. (1904).

State v. Adams Lumber Co., 81 Neb. 392. (1908).

State ex rel-Durner v. Huegin, 110 Wis. 189, 85 N.W. 1046. (1901).

State v. Gannon, 75 Conn. 206. (1902).

State v. Scollard, 126 Wash. 335, 218 Pac. 224. (1923).

State v. Rowley, 12 Conn. 101. (1837).

State v. Van Pelt, 136 N.C. 633, 49 S.E. 177, 68 L.R.A. 760, 1 Ann. Cas. 495.
                (1904).

Stephens v. Mound City Liverymen & Undertakers Assn., 295 Mo. 596, 246 S.W. 40. (1922).

Straus v. American Publishers' Assn., 177 N.Y. 473, 69 N.E. 1107. (1904).

Straus v. Victor Talking Machine Co., 297 Fed. 791. (1924).

Sullivan v. Associated Bill Posters, 272 Fed. 323. (1919).

Sultan v. Star Co., 106 Misc. N.Y. 43, 174 N.Y. 52. (1919).

Tanenbaum v. N.Y. Fire Insurance Exchange, 33 Misc. (N.Y.) 134, 68 N.Y. Supp. 342. (1900).

Territory v. Long Bell Lumber Co., 22 Okla. 893. (1908).

Ulery v. Chicago Live Stock Exchange, 54 Ill. App. 233. (1894).

Union Labor Hospital Assn. Vance Redwood Lumber Co., 158 Cal. 551, 112 Pac. 886. (1910).

Union P. Coal Co. v. United States, 173 Fed. 737, 97 C.C.A. 578. (1909).

United States v. Coal Dealers' Assn., 85 Fed. 252. (1898).

United States v. Colgate & Co., 250 U.S. 300, 39 Sup. Ct. 465, 63 L. ed. 992. (1919).

United States v. Hollis, 246 Fed. 611. (1917).

United States v. King, 250 Fed. 908. (1916).

United States v. Southern California Wholesale Grocers Assn., 207 Fed. 434, (1913). 7 F. (2d) 944. (1925).

United States v. United Shoe Machinery Co., 247 U.S. 32. (1918).

United States Gypsum Co. v. Heslop, 39 F. (2d) 228. (1930).

Victor Talking Machine Co. v. Kemeny, 271 Fed. 810. (1921).

Wabash R.R. Co. v. Young, 162 Ind. 102, 69 N.E. 1003. (1904).

Walsh V. Association of Master Plumbers, 97 Mo. App. 280, 71 S.W. 455. (1902).

Welch Grape Juice Co., v. Frey & Son, 261 Fed. 68, 171 C.C.A. 664, certiorari denied, 251 U.S. 551, 40 Sup. Ct. 56, 64 L. ed. 410. (1919).

Wellington v. Small, 57 Mass. 145. (1849).

Wesley v. Native Lumber Co., 97 Misc. 814, 53 So. 346. (1910).

<u>West Va. Transportation Co. v. Standard Oil Co.</u>, 50 W. Va. 611, 40 S.E. 591
          (1902)

<u>Western Sugar Refining Co. v. Federal Trade Commission</u>, 275 Fed. 725. (1921).

<u>Whitwell v. Continental Tobacco Co.</u>, 125 Fed. 454, 60 C.C.A. 290. (1903).

<u>Wholesale Grocers Assoc. v. Federal Trade Commission</u>, 277 Fed. 657. (1922).

<u>Willis v. Muscogee Mfg. Co.</u>, 120 G. 297, 48 S.E. 177. (1904)

<u>Wills v. Central Ice & Storage Co.</u>, 39 Tex. Civ. App. 483, 88 S.W. 265.
          (1905).

-B-

<u>Adair v. United States</u>, 208 U.S. 161. (1908)

<u>Aeolian Co., v. Fischer</u>, 40 F. (2d) 189. (1930).

<u>Alco-Sander Co. v. Amalgamated Clothing Workers of America,</u> 35 F. (2nd) 203.
          (1929).

<u>American Dental Co. v. Central Dental Co.</u>, 256 Ill. App. 279. (1930).

<u>American Federation of Labor v. Buck's Stove and Range Co.</u>, 33 App., D.C. 83,
          32 L.R.A. (N.S.) 748. (1909)

<u>American Live Stock Commission Co. v. United States</u>, 28 F. (2d) 63. (1928).
          (reversed), (see: U.S. v. Am. L.C.Co. 1929) 279 U.S.
          435.

<u>American Steel Foundries v. Tri-City Council</u>, 257 U.S. 184.

<u>Anderson & L. Mfg. Co. v. Carpenters" District Council</u>, 308 Ill. 488, 139 N.
          E. 887. (1923).

<u>Arkansas Wholesale Grocers Association v. Federal Trade Commission</u>, 18 F. (2d)
          866, (27 U.S. 533). (1927).

<u>Armstrong Cork & Insulation Co. v. Walsh</u>, Mass. 177 N. E. 2. (1931).

<u>Armstrong v. Superior Court</u>, 173 Cal. 341. (1916).

<u>Associated Hat Manufacturers v. Baird-Unteidt Co.</u>, 88 Conn. 332. (1914).

<u>Auburn Draying Co. v. Wardwell</u>, 89 Misc. (N.Y.) 501, 152 N.Y. Supp. 475,
          (1915); Aff. 178 App. Div. 270, 165 N.Y. Supp. 469.
          (1917); Aff. 227 N.Y. 1, 124 N.E. 97, 6 A.L.R. 901.

Barnes & Co. A.R. v. Chicago Typographical Union #10, 232 Ill. 424, 83 N.E.
940, 14 L.R.A. (N.S.) 1018, 13 Ann. Case 54. (1908).

Barr v. Essex Trade Council, 53 N.J. Eq. 101, 30 Atl. 881. (1894).

Baush Machinery Tool Co. v. Hill, 120 N.E. (Mass.) 188. (1918).

Bayonne Textile Corp. v. American Federation of Labor Workers, 114 N.J. Eq.
30. (1933). 116 N.J. Eq. 146. (1934).

Bayer v. Brotherhood of Painters, Decorators, & Paperhangers of America, Local
301, 154 A. 759, 108 N.J. Eq. 257. (1931).

Beaton v. Farrant, 102 Ill. App. 124. (1902).

Beattie v. Callanan, 82 App. Div. (N.Y.) 7, 81 N.Y. Supp. 413. (1903).

Beck v. Railway Teamsters' Protective Union, 118 Mich. 497, 77 N.W. 13,
42 L.R.A. 407, 74 Am. St. Ry. 421. (1898).

Beckerman v. Bakery Union, 28 Ohio N.P. (W.S.) 550. (1931).

Bedford Cut Stone Co. v. Journeymen Stone Cutters' Association, 9 Fed. (2d)
40 rev. 274 U.S. 37. (1927).

Berger v. Superior Court, 175 Cal. 719. (1917).

Berry v. Donovan, 188 Mass. 353, 74 N.E. 603. (1905).

Binkley v. United States, 282 Fed. 244. (1922).

Blandford v. Duthie, 147 Md. 388, 128 Atl. 138. (1925).

Bomés v. Providence Local No. 223 of Motion Picture Machine Operators of U.S.
and Canada, (R.I.) 155 A. 581. (1931).

Booker & Kinnaird v. Louisville Board of Fire Underwriters, 188 Ky. 771, 224
S.W. 451. (1920). (Read case re: Conspiracy v. Boycott
Important).

Booth v. Burgess, 72 N.J. Eq. 181, 65 Atl. 226. (1906).

Borden's Farm Products Co. v. Stebinsky, 117 Misc. 585, 192 N.Y.S. 727. (1922).

Bossert v. Dhuy, 221 N.Y. 342, 117 N.E. 582. (1917).

Bossert v. United Brotherhood, 77 Misc. (N.Y.) 592, 137 N.Y. Supp. 321. (1912).

Boutwell v. Marr, 71 Vt. 1, 42 Atl. 607. (1896).

Brace Bros. v. Evans, 5 Pa. Co. Ct. 163. (1888).

Brooklyn United Theater v. International Alliance of Theatrical Stage
Employees, 248 N.Y.S. 623. (1931).

Bricklayers, Masons & Plasterers International Union v. Seymour Ruff & Sons,
          160 Maryland 483, 154 A. 52 ,(1931). (See 163 Md.
          687.)

Brown v. Jacobs Pharmacy, 115 Ga. 429, 41 S.E. 553. (1902).

Buchanan v. Kerr, 159 Pa. 433, 28 Atl. 195. (1894).

Buck's Stove and Range Co. v. Gompers, 221 U.S. 418.

Bull v. International Alliance, 119 Kan. 713, 241 Pac. 459. (1925).

Burgess Bros. Co. v. Stewart, 112 Misc. (N.Y.) 347, 184 N.Y. Supp. 1991.
          (1920).

Burnham v. Dowd, 217 Mass. 351, 104 N.E. 831. (1914).

Burt v. State, 159 Ala. 134, 48 So. 851. (1909).

Butterrick Pub. Co. v. Typographical Union, 50 Misc. (N.Y.) 1, 100 N.Y.
          Supp. 292. (1906).

Buyer v. Guillian, 271 Fed. 65. (1921).

Campbell v. Motion Picture Machine Operators' Union, 151 Minn. 220, 186 N.W.
          781. (1922).

Carlson v. Carpenters' Contractors Association, 305 Ill. 331, 137 N.E. 222.
          (1922).

Carpenters' Union v. Citizens' Council, to enforce Landis Award; 333 Ill.
          225, 164 N.E. 393. (1928). (Reversing 244 Ill.
          App. 540.)

Casey v. Cincinnati Typographical Union, 45 Fed. 135, 12 L.R.A. 193. (1891).

Central Metal Products Corp. v. O'Brien, 278 Fed. 827. (1922).

City of St. Louis v. Gloner, 210 Mo. 502. (1908).

Clark Lunch Co. v. Cleveland Waiters & Beverage Dispensers Local 106,
          154 N.E. 362, 22 Ohio App. 266. (1926).

Cohen v. United Garment Workers, 35 Misc. (N.Y.) 748, 72 N.Y. Supp. 341.
          (1901).

Cohn, The & R. Electric Co. v. Bricklayers, Masons, & Plasterers Local Union,
          92 Conn. 161, 101 Atl. 659. (1917).

Commercial House & Window Cleaning Co. v. Awerkin, 240 N.Y.S. 797. (1930).

Conners v. Connelly, 86 Conn. 641. (1913).

Cook v. Wilson, 108 Misc. (N.Y.) Supp. 463. (1919).

Cooks, Waiters & Waitresses Union v. Papageorge, (Texas) 230 S.W. 1086.
          (1921).

Corcoran v. National Telephone Co., 176 Fed. 761. (1909).

Cote v. Murphy, 159 Pa, 420, 28 Atl. 190. (1894).

Crouch v. Central Labor Council of Portland and Vicinity, 293 P. 729,
                134 Or. 612. (1930).

Crump v. Commissioners, 84 Va. 927, 6 S.E. 620, 10 Am. St. Ry. 895. (1888).

Cushman's Sons v. Amalgamated Food Workers Bakers' Local, 127 Misc. (N.Y.)
                52, 215 N.Y. Supp. 401. (1926).

Curran v. Galen, 152 N.Y. 33. (1897).

Dail Overland Co. v. Willys Overland, 263 Fed. 171 (f. 274 Fed. 86).

Daitch & Co. v. Retail Grocery & Dairy Clerks Union of Greater New York,
                221 N.Y.S. 446, 129 Misc. Rep. 343. (1927).

Danz v. American Federation of Musicians, 133 Wash. 186, 233 Pac. 630.
                (1925).

Davis v. Chicago Typographical Union, 232 Ill. 420. (1912).

Davis v. State, 200 Ind. 88. (1928).

Davitt v. American Bakers Union, 124 Cal. 99, 56 Pac. 775. (1899).

Dayton Mfg. Co. v. Metal Polishers B.P. & B. Workers Union, 11 Ohio S. & C.P.
                Dec. 613. (1901).

De Agostina v. Holmden, 285 N.Y.S. 909, (1935).

Delan v. Hotel and Restaurant Employment, etc., 159 So. 637(La.) (1935).

Delz v. Winfree, 80 Tex. 400, 16 S.W. 111. (1891).

Deminico v. Craig, 207 Miss. 523, 24 N.E. 317. (1911).

Doremus v. Hennessy, 176 Ill. 608, 52 N.E. 924, 43 L.R.A. 797, 68 Am. St.
                Ry. 203. (1898).

Duplex Printing Co. v. Deering, 254 U.S. 433, 41 Sup. Ct. 172, 65 L. ed. 341.
                (1921). rev. 252 Fed. 722, 164 C.C.A. 562. (1918).
                which aff. 247 Fed. 192. (1917).

Edelman, Edelman & Berrie v. Retail Grocery & Dairy Clerks' Union, 119 Misc.
                (N.Y.) 618, 198 N.Y. Supp. 17. (1922).

Edelstein v. Gillmore, 35 F. (2d) 723. (1929).

Ellis v. Journeymen Barbers' International Union, 144 Iowa 117, 191 N.W. 111.
                (1922).

Empire Theater Co. v. Cloke, 53 Mont. 183, 163 Pac. 107. (1917).

Employee Printers' Club v. Dr. Blosser Co., 122 Ga. 509, 69 A.L.R. 90.
            (1905).

Engelmeyer v. Simon, 265 N.Y.S. 636. (1933).

Erdman v. Mitchell, 207 Pa. St. 79. (1903).

Esco v. Kaplan, 258 N.Y.S. 240. (1932).

Escanaba Mfg, Co. v. Trades and Labor Council, 160 Mich. 656. (1910).

Exchange Bakery & Restaurant v. Rifkin, 157 W.E. 130, 245 NY. 360. (1927).
                (reversing 215 N.Y.S. 753). (reargument denied 245
                N.Y. 651).

Ex Parte Sweitzer, 130 Okla. Cr. 154. (1917).

Farmers' Loan & Trust Co. v. Northern Pacific R.R. Co., 60 Fed. 803. (1894).

Federal Hats v. Golden, 226 N.Y.S. 747, 223 App. Div. 701. (1928).

Fenske Bros. v. Upholsterers' International Union, 358 Ill. 239. (1935).

Fink v. Butchers' Union, 84 N.J. Eq. 638, 95 Atl. 182. (1915).

Folsom Engraving Co. v. McNeil, 235 Mass. 269, 126 N.E. 479. (1920).

Foster v. Retail Clerks' Int, Protective Association, 39 Misc. (N.Y.) 48,
                78 N.Y. Supp. 860. (1902).

Frank & Dugan, N. v. Herold, 63 N.J. Eq. 443.

Franklin Union No.4 v. People, 220 Ill. 355, 76 N.E. 176. (1906).

Freed R.A. & Co. v. Doe, 278 N.Y.S. 68. (1935).

Garrigan v. United States, 163 Fed. 16 (214 U.S. 514). (1908).

Gevas v. Greek Restaurant Workers Club, 134 Atl. 309 (N.J. Ch.) (1925).

Gill Engraving Co. v. Doerr, 214 Fed. 111. (1914).

Godin v. Niebuhr, 236 Mass. 350, 128 N.E. 406. (1920).

Goldberg, B. & Co. v. Stablemens' Union Local No. 8760, 149 Calif. 429,
                86 Pac. 806. (1906).

Goldman v. Cohen, 227 N.Y.S. 311, 222 App. Div. 631. (1928).

Grandview Dairy v. O'Leary, 285 N.Y.S. 841. (1936).

Grassi Contracting Co. v. Bennett, 174 N.Y. App. Div. 244. (1916).

Gray v. Building Trades Council, 91 Minn. 171, 97 N.W. 663, 63 L.R.A. 753,
                103 Am. St. Rep. 477. (1903).

Greenfield v. Central Labor Council, 104 Or. 236, 192 Pac. 783, 207 Pac.
                168. (1922).

Grimes v. Durnin, 80 N.H. 143, 114 Atl. 273. (1921).

Hagan v. Blindell, 56 Fed. 696 (affirming 54 Fed. 40). (1893).

Hammer v. Baum, 240 N.Y.S. 145, 136 Misc. Rep. 940. (1930).

Hanson v. Innis, 211 Mass. 301, 97 N.E. 756. (1912).

Harvey v. Chapman, 226 Mass. 191, 115 N.E. 304. (1917).

Heffron, In re, 179 Mo. App. 639, 162 S.W. 652. (1914).

Heitkamper v. Hoffman, 99 Misc. (N.Y.) 543, 154 N.Y. Supp. 533. (1917).

Henrici, Philip Co. v. Alexander, 198 Ill App. 568. (1916).

Herzog v. Cline, Kimbery & Wasserman, 227 N.Y.S. 462, 131 Misc. Rep. 816.
                (1928).

Hitchman Coal & Coke Co. v. Mitchell, 243 U.S. 229. (1917).

Hopkins v. Oxley Stove Co., 83 Fed. 912, 28 C.C.A. 99. (1897).

Hotel & R. News Co. v. Clark, 243 Mass. 317, 137 N.E. 534. (1922).

Hughes v. Kansas City Motion Picture Machine Operatores Local, 282 Mo. 304,
                221 S.W. 95. (1920).

Illinois Central R.R. Co. v. International Association of Machinists, 190
                Fed. 910. (1911).

Interborough Rapid Transit Co. v. Lavin, 159 N.E. 863, 247 N.Y. 65 (reversing
                order 222 N.Y.S. 825, 220 App. Div. 83). (1923).

International & G.N.R. Co. v. Greenwood, 2 Tex. Cix. App. 76, 21 S.W. 559.
                (1893).

International Brotherhood E. W. v. Western Union Tel. Co., 6 F. (2nd) 444.
                (1925).

International Pocketbook Workers' Union v. Orlove, 148A. 826, 158 Ind. 496.
                (1930).

Iron Molders' Union v. Allis-Chalmers Co., 166 Fed. 45, 91 C.C.A. 631.
                (1908).

Irving v. Joint District Council, 180 Fed. 896. (1910).

Irving v. Neal, 209 Fed. 471. (1913).

Iverson v. Dilno, 44 Mont. 270, 119 Pac. 719. (1911).

Jacobs v. Cohen, 183 N.Y. 208. (1905).

Jensen v. Cooks' & Waiters' Union, 39 Wash. 531, 81 Pac. 1069. (1905).

Jetton-Dekle Lumber Co. v. Mather, (6 A.L.R. 921) 53 Fla. 969, 43 So. 590.
          (1907).

J.H. & S. Theater v. Fay, 260 N.Y. 315. (1932).

Jonas Glass Co. v. Glass Bottle Association, 72 N.J. Eq. 653, (77 N.J. Eq. 219).
          (1907).

Jones v. E. Van Winkle Gin & Mach. Wkrs., 131 Ga. 336, 62 S.E. 236. (1908).

Jordahl v. Haydn, 1 Cal. App. 696, 82 Pac. 1079. (1905).

Kemp v. Division No. 241, 255 Ill. 213, 99 N.E. 389. (1912).

Kirmse v. Adler, 311 Pa. 78. (1933).

Korges Furniture Co. v. Amalgamated Wood Workers, 165 Md. 421, 75 N.E. 877,
          2 L.R.A. 788. (1905).

Kroger Grocery & Baking Co. v. Retail Clerks' Int. Protective Assn., 250
          Fed. 890.

Lawlor v. Loewe, 235 U.S. 522, 35 Sup. Ct. 170, 59 L. ed. 341. (1915).
          affirming 209 Fed. 721, 126 C.C.A. 445. (1913).

Levering & Garrigues Co. v. Norrin, 61 F. (2d) 115, reversing (N.Y.) 1929.
          11 Law and Labor 245. (1932). See also Law and Labor
          45 F. (2d) 399. (1930).

Lindsay & Co. v. Montana Federation of Labor, 37 Mont. 264, 96 Pac. 127,
          18 L.R.A. (N.S.) 707, 127 Am. St. Rep. 722. (1908).

Lisse v. Local Union No. 31 Cooks, etc., 24 P. (2d) 833. (Cal.) (1933).

Local Union No. 313 v. Stahakis, 135 Ark. 86, 205 S.W. 450. (1918).

Loewe v. Calif. State Federation of Labor, 139 Fed. 71. (1905).

Loewe v. Lawlor, 208 U.S. 274, 28 Sup. Ct. 301, 52 L. ed. 488. (1908).

Lohse Patent Door Co. v. Fuello, 215 Mo. 421, 114 S.W. 997, 22 L.R.A. (N.S.)
          607, 128 Am. St. Rep. 492. (1908).

Loizeaux Lumber Co. v. Carpenters and Joiners Local of Roselle, (N.J. Ch.)
5 Law & Labor 250. (1923).

Longshore Printing Co. v. Howell, 26 Or. 527, 38 Pac. 547. (1894).

Lucke v. Clothing Cutters' Assembly, 77 Md. 396. (1893).

Lundoff-Bicknell Co. v. Smith, 240 App. 294. (1927).

Maisel v. Sigman, 123 Misc. (N.Y.) 714, 205 N.Y. Supp. 807. (1924).

Manker v. Bakers' Confectioners' & Waiters International Union of America,
Local 144, 221 N.Y.S. 106, 129 Misc. Rep. 516. (1927).

March v. Bricklayers' & Plasterers' Union etc., 79 Conn. 7, 63 Atl. 291.
(1906).

Martell v. White, 185 Mass. 255, 64 N.E. 1085. (1904).

Martin v. Francke, 227 Mass. 272, 116 N.E. 404. (1917).

Martin v. McFall, 65 N.J. Eq. 91. (1903).

Marx & H. Jeans Clothing Co. v. Watson, 168 Mo. 133, 67 S.W. 391. (1902).

Matthews v. Shankland, 25 Misc. (N.Y.) 604, 56 N.Y. Supp. 123. (1898).

Mayo v. Dean, 82 F. (2d) 554. (Affirming 9 F. Supp. 459). (1936).

McCord v. Thompson-Starrett Co., 129 App. Div. 130. (Aff'd 198 N.Y. 587).
(1908).

McCourtuly v. United States, 291 Fed. 497. (1923).

McCormick v. Local Union 216, 32 Ohio C.C. 165. (1911).

McGobbong v. Lancaster, 286 Fed. 129. (1923).

McGrath v. Norman, 223 N.Y.S. 228, 221 App. Div. 804. (1927).

Mears Slayton Lumber Co. v. District Council of Chicago of United Brotherhood
of Carpenters and Joiners of America, 156 Ill. App.
327. (1910).

Meier v. Spear, 96 Ark. 618, 132 S.W. 988, 32 L.R.A. (N.S.) 792. (1910).

Myers v. United States, 264 U.S. 95. (1924).

Michaels v. Hillman, 112 Misc. (N.Y.) 395, 183 N.Y. Supp. 195. (1920).

Mills v. United States Printing Co., 99 App. Div. (N.Y.) 605, 91 N.Y. Supp.
185. (1904).

Montgomery v. Pacific El. Ry. Co., 258 Fed. 392. (1919).

Moores v. Bricklayers' Union, 10 Ohio Dec. Reprint 665. (1889).

Moore v. Cooks', Waiters' & Waitresses' Union, 39 Cal. App. 538, 179 Pac.
        417. (1919).

Moran v. Lasette, 223 N.Y.S. 283, 221 App. Div. 118. (1927).

Moreland Theaters v. Portland Etc. Union, 12 P. (2d) 333. (Or.). (1932).

Mulholland v. Waiters' Local Union, 13 Ohio S. & C.P. Dec. 342. (Ohio
        Dec. N.P.). (1902).

Music Hall Theater v. Moving Picture Mach. Oper. Local No. 165, 249 Ky.
        639. (1933).

My Maryland Lodge v. Adt., 100 Md. 238, 59 Atl. 721. (1905).

N.&R. Theaters v. Basson, 127 Misc. (N.Y.) 271, 215 N.Y. Supp. 157. (1925).

Nann v. Raimist, 174 N.E. 690, 255 N.Y. 307 (Aff'g 241 N.Y.S. 832, 228
        App. Div. 856). (1931).

National Protective Assn. v. Cumming, 170 N.Y. 315, 63 N.E. 369. (1902).

Neal v. Hutcheson, 160 N.Y.S. 1007. (1916).

New England Cement Gun Co. v. McGivern, 218 Mass. 198, 105 N.E. 885. (1914).

Newark Morning Ledger Co. v. Suburban Newsdealers' Assn. of the Oranges,
        154 A. 534, 9 N.J. Misc. R. 373. (1931).

Newton v. Erickson, 70 Misc. (N.Y.) 291, 126 NY. Supp. 949. (1911).

Newton v. Laclede Steel Co., 80 F.(2d) 636. (1936).

New York Lumber Trade Assn. v. Lacey, 277 N.Y.S. 519. (1935).

O'Brien v. People, 216 Ill 354 ex rel. Kellogg Switch H. I. Supply Co. (1905).

Old Dominion S.S. Co. v. McKenna, 30 Fed. 48. (1887).

Overland Pub. Co. v. Union Lithograph Co., 57 Calif. App. 366, 207 Pac.
        412. (1922).

Overseas Storage Co. v. Chlopsek, 209 App. Div. (N.Y.) 834, 204 N. Y. Supp.
        845. (1924).

Oxley Stove Co. v. Coopers' International Union, 72 Fed. 695. (1896).

Paine Lumber Co. v. Neal, 244 U.S. 459, 37 Sup. Ct. 718, 61 L. ed. 1256.
        (1917).

Paramount Enterprises v. Mitchell, 104 Fla. 407, 140 So. 328. (1932).

Park, J. D. & Sons Co. v. National Wholesale Druggists' Assn., 175 N.Y. 1,
        67 N.E. 136. (1903).

<u>Parker Paint & Wallpaper Co. v. Local Union No. 813</u>, 87 W. Va. 651,
105 S.E. 911. (1921).

<u>Parkinson J. F. Co. v. Building Trades Council</u>, 154 Calif. 381, 96 Pac. 1027.
(1908).

<u>Patch, F.R. Mfg. Co. v. Protection Lodge</u>, 77 Vt. 294, 60 Atl. 74. (1905).

<u>Patterson v. Building Trades Council</u>, 11 Pa. Dist. R. 500. (1902).

<u>People v. Armentrout</u>, 118 Cal. App. 761, Calif. Sup. 170, 1 Fed. (2nd) 556.
(1931).

<u>People v. Davis</u>, 159 App. Div. (N.Y.) 464, 144 N.Y. Supp. 284. (1913).

<u>People v. Hughes</u>, 137 N.Y. 29, 32 N.E. 1105. (1893).

<u>People ex rel. Stearns v. Barr,</u> 181 N.Y. 462. (1905).

<u>People v. Kostka,</u> 4 N.Y. Crim. Rep. 429. (1886).

<u>People v. McFarlin</u>, 43 Misc. (N.Y.) 591, 89 N.Y. Supp. 527. (1904).

<u>People v. Nadt,</u> 15 N.Y. Crim. Rep. 174, 71 N.Y.Supp. 846. (1900).

<u>People v. Hilzig</u>, 4 N.Y. Crim. Rep. 403. (1886).

<u>Piano & O. Workers Int. Union v. Piano & O. Supply Co</u>., 124 Ill. App. 357.
(1906).

<u>Pickett v. Walsh</u>, 192 Mass. 572, 73 N.E. 753. (1906).

<u>Pierce v. Stablemens' Union Local 8760</u>, 156 Calif. 70, 103 Pac. 324. (1909).

<u>Plant v. Woods</u>, 176 Mass. 492, 57 N.E. 1011. (1900).

<u>Pleaters' & Stitchers' Assn. v. Taft</u>, 227 N.Y.S. 185, 131 Misc. Rep. 506.
(1928).

<u>Pre'Catalan v. Int. Federation of Workers</u>, 114 Misc. (N.Y.) 662, 188 N.Y.
Supp. 29. (1921).

<u>Public Baking Co. v. Stern</u>, 127 Misc. (N.Y.) 229, 215 N.Y. Supp. 537.
(1926).

<u>Puget Sound Traction L. & P. Co. v. Lawrey</u>, 202 Fed. 263. (1913).

<u>Purvis v. Local No. 500, U.B.C.J.</u>, 214 Pa. 348, 63 Atl. 585. (1906).

<u>R. & N. Hat Shop v. Sculley</u>, 98 Conn. 1, 118 Atl. 55. (1922).

<u>Reardon v. Caton</u>, 189 App. Div. (N.Y.) 501, 178 N.Y. Supp. 713. (1919).
reversing 107 Misc. 541, 177 N.Y. Supp. 803. (1919).

Reardon v. International Mercantile Marine Co., 189 App. Div. (N.Y.)515, 178 N.Y. Supp. 722. (1919).

Reynolds v. Davis, 198 Mass. 294, 84 N.E. 457. (1908).

Richter Bros. v. Journeymen Tailors' Assn., 11 Ohio Dec. Rep. 45. (1890).

Riggs v. Cincinnati Waiters' Alliance, 5 Ohio N.R. 386, 8 Ohio S. & C.P. Dec. 565. (1898).

Robinson v. Hotel & Restaurant Employees Local, 35 Ida. 418, 207 Pac. 132. (1922).

Rocky Mt. Bell Tel. Co. v. Montana F. of L., 136 Fed. 809. (1907).

Roddy v. United Line Workers, 41 Okla. 621. (1914).

Root v. Anderson, (Mo.) 207 S.W. 255. (1918).

Roosevelt Amusement v. Empire State etc. Union, 258 N.Y.S. 240. (1932).

Roraback v. Motion Picture Machine Operators Union, 140 Minn. 481, 168 N.E. 766. (1918).

Rosenberg v. Retail Clerks' Assn., 39 Cal. App. 67, 177 Pac. 854. (1918).

Ruff, Seymour & Sons v. Bricklayers', etc. Union, 163 Mo. 687. (1933).

Sackett, etc. Co. v. National Association, N.Y. 61 Misc. 150. (1898).

Sailors' Union v. Hammond Lumber Co., 156 Fed. 450. (1907).

St. Germaine v. Bakery & C. Workers Int. Union, 97 Wash. 282, 166Pac. 665. (1917).

Sarros v. Nouris, 138 A. (Del. Ch.) 607. (1927).

Schlang v. Ladies' Waist Makers' Union, 67 Misc. (N.Y.) 221, 124 N.Y. Supp. 289. (1910).

Scofer, et. al. v. Helmar, 205 Ind. 596, 187 N.E. 662 (Ind.) (1933).

Schwartz v. Benjamin, 246 N.Y.S. 419, 138 Misc. Rep. 917. (1931).

Scott-Stafford Opera House Co. v. Minneapolis Musicians Assoc., 118 Minn. 410, 136 N.W. 1092. (1912).

Searle Mfg. Co. v. Terry, 56 Misc. (N.Y.) 265, 104 N.Y. Supp. 438. (1907).

Searle Mfg. Co. v. Terry, et. al., 106 N.Y. Supp. 438, 56 Misc. 265. (1905).

Seattle Brewing & Malting Co. v. Hansen, 144 Fed. 1011. (1905).

Seubert v. Reiff, 98 Misc. (N.Y.) 402, 164 N.Y. Supp. 522. (1917).

Service Wood Heel Co. v. Mackesy, 199 N.E. 400 (Mass). (1936).

Shaughnessy v. Jordan, 184 Ind. 499. (1916).

Sherry v. Perkins, 147 Mass. 212, 17 N.E. 307. (1888).

Shine v. Fox Bros. Mfg. Co., 156 Fed. 557, 86 C.C.A. 311. (1907).

Sinsheimer v. United Garment Workers, 77 Hun. (N.Y.) 215, 28 N.Y. Supp.
          321. (1894).

Smith v. Bowen, 121 N.E. (Mass.) 814. (1919).

Snow, W.A., Iron Works, Inc. v. Chadwick, 227 Mass. 382. (1917).

Springfield Spinning Co. v. Riley, L.R. 6 Equity 551. (1868).

State v. Bittner, 102 W, Va. 677. (1926).

State v. Employers of Labor, 102 Neb. 768. (1918).

State v. Clidden, 55 Conn. 46, 8 Atl. 890, 3 Am. St. Rep. 23. (1887).

State ex rel. Lindsley v. Grady, 114 Wash. 692. (1921).

State v. McGee, 80 Conn. 614, 69 A. 1059, 81 Conn. 696. (1908).

State v. Stewart, 59 Vt. 273. (1887).

State v. Stockford, 77 Conn. 227, 58 Atl. 769. (1904).

Stearns, A.T. Lumber Co. v. Howlett, 260 Mass. 45, 157 N.E. 82. (1927).

Steffes v. Motion Picture Machine Operators Union, 136 Minn. 200, 161 N.W.
          524. (1917).

Steinert M. & Sons Co. v. Fagen, 207 Mass. 394, 93 N.E. 584. (1911).

Steinkritz Amusement Corp. v. Kaplan, 248 N.Y.S. 624. (1931).

Stewart v. United States, 236 Fed. 838. (1916).

Stillwell Theater v. Kaplan, 249 N.Y.S. 122. (1931).

Stillwell Theater v. Kaplan, 259 N.Y. 405. (1932).

Stout, ex parte, 82 Tex. Crim. Rep. 183, 198 S.W. 967. (1917).

Sumwalt Ice Co. v. Knickerbocker Ice Co., 114 Md. 403. (1911).

Swartz v. Kay, 89 W. Va. 641, 109 S.E. 832. (1921).

Thomas v. Cincinnati, N.O. & T.P.R. Co., 62 Fed. 803. (1894).

Thomas v. Indianapolis, 195 Ind. 440, 145 N.E. 550. (1924).

Thomson Machine Co. v. Brown, 89 N.J. 326, 104 Atl. 129, 108 Atl. 116. (1918).

Toledo, S.A. & N.R.R. Co. v. Pennsylvania Co., 54 Fed. 730, 19 L.R.A. 387. (1893).

Tosa v. West Kentucky Coal Co., 252 Fed. 44. (1918).

Traub Amusement Co. v. Hacker, 127 Misc. (N.Y.) 335, 215 N.Y. Supp. 397. (1925).

Trade Press Pub. Co. v. Milwaukee Typographical Union, 180 Mis. 449. (1923).

Tree-Marx Shoe Co. v. Schwartz, 248 N.Y.S. 56, 139 Misc. Rep. 136. (1931).

Truax v. Bisbee Local No. 380 C.T.U., 19 Ariz. 379, 171 Pac. 121. (1918).

Truax v. Corrigan, 257 N.E. 312, 42 Sup. Ct. 124, 661 Fed. 254. (1921).

Trustees of Wis. St. Federation of Labor v. Simplex Shoe Mfg. Co., 256 N.W. 56 (Wis.). (1934).

Underhill v. Murphy, 117 Ky. 640, 78 S.W. 482. (1904).

United Chain Theaters v. Philadelphia Moving Picture Machine Operators Union, Local No. 307, U.S. D.C. Pa. 50 F. (2d) 189. (1931).

United States v. Atler, 62 Fed. 324. (1894).

United States v. Brims, 6 F. (2d) 98, (1928); rev. 47 Sup. Ct. 189. (1926).

United States v. American Livestock Commission Co., A. 5 Ct. 475, 279 U.S. 435, 73 L. ed. 787 (rev. 28 F. (2d) 63, Amer. Live. Comm. Co. v. U.S.). (1929).

United States v. Needle Traders' Workers' Union, 10 F. Supp. 201. (1935).

United States v. Morris, 255 Fed. 423. (1918).

United States v. Raish, 163 Fed. 911. (1908).

Vaughan v. Kansas City Moving Picture Machine Operators Union Local No. 170, 36 F. (2d) 78. (1930).

Vegilahn v. Gunther, 167 Miss. 92. (1896).

Vonderschmitt v. McGuire, 193 N.E. 385 (Ind.). (1935).

Vonnegut Machinery Co. v. Toledo Machine & Tool Co., 263 Fed. 192. (1920).

Waler v. Cronin, 107 Mass. 555. (1871).

Walton Lunch Co. v. Kearney, 236 Mass. 310, 128 N.E. 429. (1920).

Waterhouse v. Coker, 35 Fed. 149. (1893).

Walters v. Retail Clerks' Union No. 473, 120 Va. 424, 47 S.E. 911. (1904).

Wann v. Aijist, 255 N.Y. 308. (1931).

Webb v. Cooks', Waiters' & Waitresses' Union, (Texas) 205 S.W. 463. (1913).

Webb v. Drake, 32 Ia. Ann. 290, 26 So. 791. (1899).

Wilcutt & Sons Co. v. Driscoll, 200 Mass. 110, 85 N.E. 297. (1908).

Willner v. Silverman, 109 Fed. 341, 71 W. 962, 24 N.S. 895. (1909).

Willow Cafeteria v. Kramberg, 237 N.Y.S. 76, 184 Misc. Rep. 841. (1929).

Wilson v. Hay, 232 Ill. 389, 83 N.E. 928. (1906).

Willson & Adams Co. v. Pearce, 237 N.Y.S. 601, 135 Misc. Rep. 426. (1930).

Willson & Adams Co. v. Pearce, 265 N.Y.S. 624, 240 App. Div. 718. (1933).

Wise Shoe v. Lowenthal, 206 N.Y. 264. (1935).

Wyeman v. Ready, 79 Conn. 414, 63 Atl. 129. (1906).

Yablowitz v. Horn, 305 App. Div. (N.Y.) 440, 199 N.Y. Supp. 769. (1923).

Yates Hotel Co. v. Meyers, 195 N.Y. Supp. 558. 192

York Mfg. Co. v. Cherdick, 10 Pa. Dist N. 463. (1901).